Deborah,

God's Best...

He loves you,

Eph. 3:20-21

Thrill helps expose the lies of our enemy, illustrating those deceptions with stories from Karl's life and the lives of those he has touched. I for one am thankful that Karl wrote this book. My life is richer and my dreams are higher because of it. You and I were made for a thrilling adventure in life! Join Karl as he leads us to go where our Father wants us to go and be what He wants us to be.

— **Dr. John Jackson**, Executive Director,
Thriving Churches International

Karl Clauson was my pastor for nearly a decade — and I was always challenged by his sermons. Karl has a knack for communicating familiar truth in a fresh, creative way — and that's exactly what he's done in this book.

— **David Murrow**, bestselling author of *Why Men Hate Going to Church*

Clauson's book, *Thrill*, takes a refreshingly honest look at the struggle to find true faith and the "contagious" life. His accounts of both his successes and failures on the journey give hope to all who struggle with "performing" to gain God's acceptance. He describes the "black holes" of life as those agonizing periods of waiting that sometimes precede God's deliverance. In this book, you will find a genuine fellow traveler on the faith journey. He is sometimes successful, sometimes not, but always counting on God's grace to inhabit the "Black holes of life — even when we cannot see Him or find Him."

— **Paul Eshleman**, Vice President of Campus Crusade for Christ

Thrill challenged, convicted, and compelled me to re-examine all the rooms in my soul, all the drawers in my chest, and all the secrets in my safe. This book provides a powerful clot buster for removing any of Thrill Killer's attempts to clog and block our spiritual arteries. Read Karl's story and never settle for "normal" again.

— **Billy Browning**, PhD, Organizational Psychologist

Who Karl Clauson is comes out in every line of this book. Normal is killing our country, our city, our families, and us. Karl has articulated the path out of this valley of the shadow of death. Purchase two copies of this book, one for yourself and one for someone you love dearly.

—**Dean Curry**, Senior Pastor,
Life Center, Tacoma, Washington

There is honesty and freshness about *Thrill: When Normal Is Not Enough* that rings with authenticity about the author himself. Karl has described the trials and triumphs of the Christian life in such a way as to keep the reader fascinated and wanting more. This book will lead many unbelievers to Christ and cause many believers to make deeper commitments to intimacy with the Savior.

—**Dr. Norm Cook**, International Ministry Team, OC International
—**Muriel Cook**, Counselor-at-Large, Multnomah University

Thrill is just a taste of Karl's pure passion for people to know God and experience authentic faith. I've witnessed the impact of Karl's gifting as he led a dynamic, culture-changing church. Now many others get a chance to experience what my friend brings to the table of God's kingdom work.

—**Kirk Nowery**, COO Samaritans Purse

There is a hard reality that many of us in the church do not want to face—the very people who say they have new life in Christ are settling for less than what He promises and gives. The thrill is gone for so many—and the world has taken notice. In *Thrill: When Normal Is Not Enough*, Karl Clauson champions a vision of what Christ promised and truly delivers. If you are tired of settling and want to be stirred up with fresh vision for what life in Christ was meant to be, then I highly recommend you make this your next read.

—**Tim Lundy**, Directional Leader,
Fellowship Bible Church, Little Rock, Arkansas

THRILL

WHEN **NORMAL** IS NOT **ENOUGH**

KARL CLAUSON

credo
house publishers

Thrill: When Normal Is Not Enough
Copyright © 2010 Karl Clauson
All rights reserved.

Published by Credo House Publishers, a division
of Credo Communications, LLC, Grand Rapids, Michigan;
www.credocommunications.net.

ISBN-10: 1-935391-48-8
ISBN-13: 978-1-935391-48-7

Scripture is taken from The Holy Bible, English Standard Version,
copyright © 2001 by Crossway Bibles, a division of Good News Publishers.
Used by permission. All rights reserved.

Cover design: PlainJoe Studios
Interior design: Frank Gutbrod

Printed in the United States of America

To Junanne —
My bride, encourager and best friend.
You never settle for normal.

To Kaben and Muriel —
Two of the most dynamic thrill seekers
a dad could ever have.

To Dad and Mom —
Your love for God and people is the real deal.

To Marvin Smith —
Your friendship to me and my family
is extraordinary.

ACKNOWLEDGMENTS

So many special people have contributed to this book. I don't have space to name you all, but I do want to single out for my thanks:

Lifelane180 Board of Directors and wives—You men and women are uniquely equipped gifts from God.

Elevate Consulting—Jake, your skillful writing is superseded only by your depth of character.

Bethany Felix—The way you think and edit brings light and fresh air to the world.

Mike Hamel—You brought wisdom and expertise just when we needed it.

Jason, Rebekah and Dan—You have lightened the load and put a smile on my face.

Tim Kimmel—You're the ultimate coach.

Many praying friends—Thanks for being at the epicenter of this project. Special thanks to Vashti and Kay.

TABLE OF CONTENTS

INTRODUCTION

I could hardly believe that Dad ordered me a large-sized root beer on my first trip to A&W on that warm summer day. And the fact that it came in a frosted / thick glass mug…oh, baby! We unwrapped our straws and plunged them in. Dad began to drink, and a look of satisfaction came over his face. I stared into my chilled root beer and tried to suck up some for myself, but nothing happened. I sucked harder still, managing to pull up what seemed to be atomized specks of root beer. It was at that point that I learned about "cracked straw syndrome." I had a barely visible crack in my straw, just above root beer line.

There's a problem in our Christian culture today. Believers have great expectations about God but aren't fully experiencing Him. The problem isn't with God. We have hairline cracks in our spiritual lives that make it impossible for us to get a deep drink of the thrilling life God offers us.

We're born with these cracks and have acquired more over the years. But there's hope. A king named David, who had plenty of cracks in his straw, once invited, "Oh, taste and see that the Lord is good!" (Psalm 34:8).

My hope is that this book seals up the cracks in your life. God wants you to get a deep draft of refreshing truth and to have a life-changing experience with Him. So plunge in and soak up all you can of God. He's so good!

ONE

THRILL SEEKERS

**I love to keep people searching for
but never experiencing real thrill.**

— Thrill Killer

In March of 1977 I listened to the finish of the Iditarod Trail
Sled Dog Race on a little AM radio. Those athletes had
raced 1,100 miles across some of Alaska's toughest terrain
in the dead of winter. I was enthralled. Although I was only
16, I began to dream big!

"This is it!" I thought. "My chance to experience something extraordinary. All I have to do is get a dog team to
Nome, Alaska!"

For the next two years I trained with focus and diligence. I took my little team of dogs and quickly expanded
it. My 20 Alaskan Husky friends and I trained hard for
the race, logging a couple of thousand miles by the time I
finished high school.

The Iditarod was first run in 1973. Its grueling course
stretches from Willow (near Anchorage) to Nome. Mush-
ers and their dog teams often race through gale-force

blizzards and sub-zero temperatures, with wind chill dropping to -100° F.

On the first Saturday in March, 1979, I arrived at the starting line with 13 incredible four-legged athletes in front of me. The next three weeks would test us as I had never before imagined or experienced. The daily routine was grueling—racing around the clock; building fires and cooking food at every stop for my dogs; checking for injuries; bedding them down on fresh straw; and then, if there was time, caring for myself—all of this in some of the harshest terrain and winter weather known to man.

After 1,100 miles on the trail, we crossed under the Burled Arch, finishing the race in 21 days, 12 hours, 8 minutes and 29 seconds. I had fought off the urge to quit, endured temperatures that froze my fingers and face, and battled sleep deprivation that caused some vivid hallucinations. But I had survived. The intense struggle was complete. Finally, I'd arrived. As an 18-year-old who'd been raised in Alaska, I had accomplished an improbable feat, and I became an instant hero in my home town.

Now for the crazy part. Only a few hours after completing the race, I was overcome by a deep sense of emptiness. I felt as though there had to be something more. That night I wandered Front Street in Nome. The bars were in full swing, but I was too young to buy a beer. I walked alone and lonely in that frozen place. I can't say I've ever heard God audibly, but that night I sensed that He was speaking to me. I struggled with a decision I had to make—to follow Him or to forge my own path. I made the wrong choice— and spent the next four years trying everything a young man could conceive to fill my God-void. Nothing worked.

Pascal talks about a God-shaped void we all have in our hearts, and I believe he's right. I had to learn that nothing on Earth can fill that vacuum but God Himself. For me, nothing worked — not finishing the Iditarod, not relationships and not parties. They all came up short. Eventually I found myself working in the oil fields of Prudhoe Bay, Alaska. I was only 19 and making good money, but had no direction in life. I started using cocaine. I was running hard — but not toward God. As I think back on those days, it's as though I were running straight into Satan's deceptive trap. I have another name for the Evil One now — Thrill Killer. I prefer to use Thrill Killer not because I think Satan or The Devil don't exist. But because I don't think most of us understand just how real our spiritual enemy is. Our problem is not that we are unaware of Satan; it's either that we've allowed him to become a mythical character who is "out there" or that we ascribe power to Satan that isn't truly his. We don't need to fear the Thrill Killer, but we must be aware of his life-stealing tactics.

BOTTOMED OUT

One dreadful winter night, several ounces of cocaine were confiscated at Anchorage International Airport. My name was on the package — or so said my friend, who tried to pick it up and instead found himself picked up by authorities. Because God is kind, I wasn't there. If I had been, I probably wouldn't be blessed today with the great gifts of my bride and children. God is often and unaccountably good to screw-ups like me, extending mercy even when we're livin' like hell.

My prayerful parents were aware of my lifestyle. In late 1983, on a visit to their lake house in Wasilla, Alaska, my dad and mom took me aside to talk with me. Both were in tears. I mentally prepared myself for their "you need to get to church" talk. But not this time. Instead they told me of their strong, felt need to pray that I would either fully surrender my life to God or be taken by Him out of this world. This ominous message shook me because for over 20 years I'd been hearing my folks asking God for things and seeing them receive tangible answers.

"... they told me of their strong, felt need to pray that I would either fully surrender my life to God or be taken by Him out of this world."

The next few months felt like a death spiral for my soul. I maximized my sin, with the result of utter emptiness. I acted as though I were full of life, while I was in reality at my lowest point ever. Broken and desperate, I went for a drive to clear my head.

What I was feeling so deeply I now refer to as the silent scream of my soul. It was on that drive that God interrupted the madness of my life. He asked me whether I was done doing things my way. I was. I don't recall my exact words, but I cried out to God to take complete control.

On February 11, 1984, God changed me. I drove to my big sister's house, walked through the front door, fell on the floor and bawled like a baby for two hours. As all the pain and regret emptied out of me, God began pouring new life into the empty space. I felt the guilt and shame leaving me as love and hope flooded in to take its place. It was as though an old Karl were dying and a new Karl was being born.

STILL CHANGING

That night the real thrill began. God performed a miracle in turning me around. He replaced destructive addictions with healthy passions. He altered my focus and gave me a vision for my future that was better than anything I'd ever dreamed. The 180-degree turn is what I'd so desperately needed in my life. I was now God's child, totally forgiven and on a path to authentic adventure!

But thrill is a journey. There are other 180-degree turns God will ask us to make along the way. On that day I had many things God needed to change in me, and He's still changing me to this day. I witnessed God's power to forgive and remake me into a better man — and He did so, through the process subjecting me to some deep — and necessary — pain. But, as I'll explain, that's all part of the thrill.

Jesus wants more than to have us make it into heaven for some eternity that hasn't yet begun. He wants to possess our hearts in the here and now, to take us on a journey that is tough, powerful, uncertain, awesome — and fills life to the max with a whole lot of joy.

Some of you don't have the real deal. Some of you, despite having been radically altered by God's goodness, are stuck once again in old patterns or lies that have you discouraged and defeated. And some of you are brimful of religion but empty of God. I've lived through all of these conditions and can testify to the exhilarating adventure of continued life-change along a path with God through a broken world.

We're all born without God. Nothing we get or do can fill our God-void. Sure, we can get religion, but religion won't get us God. We can run like hell, get changed by God and then proceed to build a life for ourselves, by ourselves. We can look like put-together professionals on the outside but never truly experience God — only cheap substitutes.

The good news is that there's hope. It comes with repenting of the life you've made for yourself and turning to Jesus. *Repentance* is one of those words Thrill Killer has twisted in his attempt to make God appear perpetually angry. In reality, the invitation to repentance is a loving, passionate invitation from God for us to turn around and join in His thrilling celebration of life (see Luke 15:23–24). The only hope there is for us is to call out to God, asking Him to do a 180 in us.

Right now, today, God is asking "Are you done yet? Are you tired of chasing your passion your own way? Are you sick of your pride? Are you done living a dual life that keeps you pretending and performing?" If you're ready for thrill, it's time to surrender everything to God. Some of you need to surrender for the first time. Others need the refreshing experience of yielding yourselves all over again. Wherever you are in life, God is waiting to accompany you on a truly fulfilling adventure.

DEATH BY NORMAL

Fear is a powerful emotion. It can keep us alive or choke the life out of us. Sometimes fear is healthy, but at other times it keeps us in a rut of doing the "normal" thing. I used to love the huge rope swing my dad built for us kids. That monster swing was like an ominous giant I just had to conquer. When Dad said "Let me push you higher," I'd agree—through clenched teeth and with a rush in my gut. Swinging so high that I was out of reach of my dad was absolutely awesome. And when I was done, I'd coax my friends to let my dad send them on the ride of their lives. Spiritually, our heavenly Father wants to send us soaring, but Thrill Killer wants us to decline the offer. When we pull back in fear of where God might be taking us, Thrill Killer wins. And we settle for normal.

Don't get me wrong, normal can be a good thing. We like blood-test results to come back normal. We like uneventful commutes on freeways. But spiritually speaking, normal is deadly. Thrill Killer has it in for us, and his weapon of choice is to tempt us with the status quo.

Thrill Killer is an ace at the comparison game. He wants us to look around and pay attention to what others are experiencing, rather than venturing into a God-sized vision for our lives. He wants us either to desire the "normal" life of others or to fear others' opinion of us so much that we design our lives to look normal. Thrill Killer threatens us with fear either of being rejected or of appearing to be crazy. After a while, Thrill Killer can switch to autopilot because normal becomes what most people both expect and experience. But in my opinion normal is an awful way to live—and die.

"Thrill Killer has it in for us, and his weapon of choice is to tempt us with the status quo."

Thrill Killer undermines us by monopolizing upon our past failures and insecurities. "You don't deserve more," he taunts. He points out our mistakes and hammers us with whispered lies: "You're damaged goods" or "The best you can expect is hanging on until heaven." It really ticks me off how he tells our seniors "The best years have passed you by" or murmurs to our vulnerable teens and young adults "Something's wrong with you." Thrill Killer is cruel, and he hits us wherever we're raw and sensitive. His intention is to shut down our initiative and exuberance and keep us, at best, inching forward in our rut.

But here's the problem: Normal isn't good enough. Buying what Thrill Killer is selling is like joining an online marketing scam selling "normal Christian living"—with the result a numbing of our spirituality. Going with the majority's predictable flow aces us out of a life that's beyond what we could ever imagine. The cost of this choice is huge. It extracts a precious price, distributed among our friendships, marriages, family lives, ministries and careers. Normal negatively impacts our overall quality of life by rendering it shallow and hollow. Normal can seem so okay, but nothing else kills the thrill like normal does.

CHOOSE LIFE

God gives us the power to choose. For millennia He's afforded people the opportunity to choose life or death (see Deuteronomy 30:19). This book is about two ways of living: the life of normal and the life of thrill. Normal is settling for the status quo. Too often we miss God's best because normal clouds our vision and dampens our souls. We become marginal or cultural Christians. We compartmentalize Jesus to a day or two a week, confine Him to "quiet times," and make of Him an acquaintance with whom we periodically touch base. We fall into patterns of thinking that church and real life are unrelated. As we start settling for normal, we ignore the subdued voice in our souls telling us that we're living a life that's less than the best. We ignore God's call to choose life.

Normal creeps into our lives like a thief. It tells us we deserve a break. So we watch television every night as a stress reliever after slaving away in jobs we neither hate nor love. Normal tells us that inaction is better than risking failure, that being a good Christian simply means going to church, donating some time or money to a good cause, praying over dinner and refraining from cheating on our spouses or drinking to excess. Normal invites us to find our "self" in sports or politics—anything other than God.

Normal doesn't get passionate about God. It cautions against going overboard, validating moderation in all things — religion in particular. Normal never changes a culture, and it has little or no eternal impact. Thrill Killer's objective is to mire us up to our armpits in normal. When normal becomes our goal, he lets us score every time.

NOT ENOUGH

Normal can be tricky. Sometimes it may look quite extraordinary, but it has a fatal flaw. The tenth chapter of Mark's Gospel shares a story that illustrates the undetected death grip normal has on our lives and souls. As the story goes, a wealthy young man walked up to Jesus and asked, "What must I do to inherit eternal life?"

Jesus looked at the young man and mouthed the answer he was probably expecting: "You know the commandments: Do not commit adultery, Do not murder, Do not steal, Do not bear false witness, Honor your father and mother."

"All right!" thinks the rich man. "I've got this in the bag." Gloating, he responds with confidence, "All these I have kept from my youth."

It's at this predictable point in the story that Scripture throws us a curve: "And Jesus, looking at him, loved him, and said to him, 'You lack one thing: go, sell all that you have and give to the poor, and you will have treasure in heaven; and come, follow me.' Disheartened by the saying, [the rich young man] went away sorrowfully, for he had great possessions" (Mark 10:21–22).

"We can make an idol of almost anything, thereby substituting a life of normalcy for what could've been a life of thrill."

Many of us read this story and think it's all about money. We assume that God equates poverty with godliness. Wrong!

The story isn't about money at all. It's about enslavement to idols. Idolatry rears its head when someone or something other than God hits our thrill button. Money was this man's idol, holding him back from risking a life of thrill. We can make an idol of almost anything, thereby substituting a life of normalcy for what could've been a life of thrill.

KILLING IDOLS

We all have idols in our lives. In the words of John Calvin, "The human heart is an idol factory…. [E]very one of us is, from his mother's womb, expert in inventing idols." Idols keep us fenced in to a normal existence, leaving us able only to peer out from our captivity toward a better life, a life of thrill. But God is continuously challenging us to tear down our idols and exchange normal for thrill. We're born into slavery to idols, but God's passion is to set us free. His Word assures us that He has much more stashed away for us, treasure infinitely more spectacular than anything we can chase in this life (see Matthew 13:44–45). When you identify your idols, lay them down, turn your back on normal and lean into God full-tilt, you participate in a breathtaking, real-life experience. Ask Him for a glimpse of His treasures, and begin to feel His thrill.

> "We need to kill our idols before they kill us."

Thrill means saying yes to God's call and no to the idols that would drag us down and hold us back. It's life lived to the fullest. It's finding friendship in God day and night and discovering, crazy as it may seem, that God fulfills our deepest passions. As David expressed it, "Delight yourself in the LORD, and he will give you the desires of your heart" (Psalm 37:4).

Here's the supreme irony: Our problem isn't that we want too much from life but that we're settling for too little.

C. S. Lewis was right on when he reflected, "Indeed, if we consider the unblushing promises of reward and the staggering nature of the rewards promised in the Gospels, it would seem that Our Lord finds our desires not too strong, but too weak. We are half-hearted creatures, fooling about with drink and sex and ambition when infinite joy is offered us, like an ignorant child who wants to go on making mud pies in a slum because he cannot imagine what is meant by the offer of a holiday at the sea. We are far too easily pleased." We need to kill our idols before they kill us.

FREEDOM

Just the other night as I was talking with my bride, Junanne, about the concept of thrill, she said something so simple and yet so profound: "Bub [that's what she calls me], I really believe that thrill, at its core, is freedom." And she's right! Thrill is the freedom to trust God so much that giving yourself over to Him is the only way to live as He created you to live. Paradoxically, this is the ultimate realization of our deepest desires…and so much more.

A life of thrill is one that gives us the freedom to pursue our passions and enjoy God's gifts and creation without trepidation—because we know and trust that He takes care of those who pursue Him (see Matthew 6:33). Thrill acknowledges that God is in control and we're not. That God has good—make that *great*—plans for us. Thrill is submitting every area of our lives to God and trusting Him as a child trusts his dad. After all, God is the consummate Daddy who's always there for us, always cheering us on. Does it surprise you to know that God wants you to win?

FIST PUMPIN' FATHER

During my sixth grade year my dad and mom made a huge personal sacrifice to pursue professional opportunities. We moved to Arizona so Dad could finish his studies for a PhD at Arizona State University. His course work was rigorous. I remember watching Dad busting it for months on end. He pulled As in everything he took. Mom worked a part-time job and lovingly typed up and proofread Dad's doctoral dissertation.

Even with insanely busy schedules, my folks made time with us kids a priority, taking time, for example, for a dip in the pool with us under the blistering Tempe sun. They made memories that stick to this day with my sisters and me.

My dad and I share a love of sports. Flag football was big in Tempe. I was a skinny but fast kid, so I jumped in and was slotted as a running back and return man. Dad tried his best to make it to my games—and, boy, did I love it when he was there.

One warm night, on a lit practice field just outside Sun Devil Stadium (I can still feel the muggy air and see the bugs under those blazing lights), we were nearing the end of a game. All we needed was one score to seal the victory. Receiving a kickoff at about the 30-yard line, I ran left. The defense bit—and I mean all of them. I reversed field and ran to the opposite side and headed up field, barely staying inbounds as I broke free past the final defender. As I was running with all my might, I looked ahead to the end zone about 50 yards away and saw my dad riding up on his bicycle. Everything moved for me into slow motion. Dad jumped off his bike, fists pumping, as I sprinted as fast as my legs would carry me toward him and the end zone. As

I crossed the goal line, I could see the uncontainable joy on his face. That moment is forever seared in my memory.

What happened in that moment in the heart of an impressionable 12-year-old boy is hard to explain. My own thrill was mirrored in my dad's joy, and his vicarious thrill was in watching me score! I ran back to celebrate with my team and coaches, but that look exchanged between my dad and me was the transcendent moment of the touchdown.

The adrenaline rush and elation of that experience are a reflection of what the synergy between our heavenly Father and each of us can be. God loves us—so much that He's fist-pumpin' excited when we score in life. We can enjoy the rush of God's pleasure in our little victories. I tell people that if they listen closely they can hear God cheering them on. So run full-tilt toward Him with everything you have (see Hebrews 12:1–2). He's waiting.

When our view of God matches the truth of God, we're freed to begin a relationship with Him that's based on friendship, not fear. When we begin to grasp the magnitude of God's love toward us, we're ready to consider the possibilities with regard to His work in us. When we understand and acknowledge that God our Father is truly for us, we can take a leap of faith to make big plays, knowing that He's there watching us with delight on His face. As the perfect Father, God reserves for us an absolute and unconditional love. As the Bible tells us, "There is no fear in love, but perfect love casts out fear" (1 John 4:18).

DON'T LET FEAR HOLD YOU BACK

I have a confession: I do battle fear. We all do. Far too often we let fear of the unknown keep us chained to a diminishing life. We're afraid to step out and try something new—

something our hearts desire so much. Instead we retreat to the safety of the certain and comfortable. But when we do that we miss out on so many great things God has for us.

"...if our motor lost power we were seconds away from certain death." There's a mighty river in the heart of Alaska called the Talkeetna. One sunny summer day I loaded my family, two coolers, and all kinds of other stuff we didn't need onto an 18-foot, four-seat, shallow-draft riverboat. The underpowered (for the river), 35-horsepower engine had a habit of breaking down. As we emerged from the slew and rounded the corner onto that raging river, I knew we were in for a dangerous, wild ride. The river was near flood stage, and the water looked as though it were boiling. I was the only one who realized we were in over our heads. It was better that way.

"What an awesome day," my wife yelled over the sound of the motor and the river pounding the bottom of the little boat. And yeah, it was awesome in many ways, what with the spacious blue sky, the lush vegetation, and crisp air filling our lungs and making us feel oh so alive! At every bend I navigated around massive logjams of 40-foot trees swept from the banks into the river—all the while knowing that if our motor lost power we were seconds away from certain death.

I prayed more passionately that day for the life of our motor than I had for the lives of most people. Every twist and turn brought another unexpected threat until, after 20 minutes of white-knuckled craziness, the river widened and the water calmed. The next few miles were relaxing and enjoyable. *How could something this beautiful*, I wondered, *be so deadly just a couple of miles back?*

Before long we arrived at a smaller stream called Clear Creek. As we pulled up, onlookers shot us stares that asked, "Did you really just come through all that stuff in *that glorified bathtub*?" I confidently jumped out in my waders, pulled the boat up on the bank and helped everyone onto the shore.

We fished for hours and had a ball. My family recognized intuitively that there had been some element of danger in the journey we'd just undertaken, but ultimately they had enjoyed the wild ride. In the face of calculated risk, they had trusted me to get them through the turbulence — and to navigate us safely to our destination.

Sure, we could've stayed home that day. It would've been safer, but imagine what we would've missed! No, I didn't purposely put my family in imminent danger, but the reality is that any time we venture beyond normal we undertake an element of risk. If we'd decided to stay home and watch TV or work around the house, the laughter, tension, exhilaration, challenge — even the moments of fear — would all have been missed.

Not all of us are wild about adventure. But each of us needs in one way or another to encounter the presence, power and deliverance of God. Each of us must initiate the thrill-experience of relinquishing our self unreservedly to our spiritual Father, trusting implicitly in his ability and desire to navigate us safely through the rapids into new territory — while we sit back and enjoy the ride alongside Him. The normal life misses out on the greatness, adventure, deep satisfaction and thrill of God. The good news is that He's inviting us even now to ditch our normal lives and join Him on a wild, thrill-filled ride.

YOUR INVITATION HAS ARRIVED

Authentic faith isn't safe. It's risky. When we put it all on the line and trust God to take us forward, He gives us a life of thrill. God becomes our source of joy, protection, provision and delight.

But let's be realistic. Thrill isn't simply synonymous with joy. Thrill is the fusion of every emotion we experience, along with every action we take, as we jump into the river with God. Trusting, fearing, shouting, wrestling, praying, cheering and reminiscing are all taste teasers of the fullness of the thrill. God has designed a unique plan and itinerary for each of us. The truth is that the thrill can be painful at times; it may in fact cause us to experience pain such as we've never even imagined. But there's overwhelming peace in knowing that we belong to God. He specializes in navigating through any suffering or challenge we might encounter. Your trip will be different from mine, and mine will be different from that of the guy on the other side, but make no mistake—He'll get each of us through because each of us has been designed for thrill!

"Your invitation to live a thrill-filled life has arrived."

If you sense that you're missing out on life, maybe you're not living up to your full, God-thrill potential. Your past may include the experience of getting swamped spiritually and having to be plucked from near death. Will you be in over your head yet again? Absolutely! But this time God—since you've joined him—will be there with you. There can be no thrill without being in over your head. You'll discover that the essence of thrill is being out of control while, paradoxically, being under God's control—which is precisely where freedom begins.

There are no shortcuts or quick fixes for opening your life to thrill, but I can promise you you'll experience the life you've been looking for. Aren't you sick yet of normal? I know I am. Normal simply isn't enough. Your invitation to live a thrill-filled life has arrived.

LIVIN' LIKE HELL

We've all heard the phrase "livin' like hell." It usually conjures up images of sleeping around, partying every night and waking up hung over just to do it all over again. What's lost in the phrase is its more universal application: "Livin' like hell" is a perfect description of life without God at its center.

We all have something dreadful in common: We're born sinners! We're out of sync with God, and we're spiritually dead. We lack the capacity to understand God, and, most importantly, we don't even seek God or the life of thrill God has for us. We're naturally selfish people who are hell-bent on making a life and making it on our own—often regardless of the cost to oth-

"If we don't have God in our sights, cheering us on, we're running in the wrong direction."

ers. The apostle Paul addresses this in his letter to the Romans: "None is righteous, no, not one; no one understands; no one seeks for God" (Romans 3:10–11).

We may try to fool ourselves into thinking we're good people. Just like the rich young man, we bust our tails trying to do things that please God. The problem is that we don't understand the real downside of sin. Sin is like a wedge for splitting wood. It puts a divide between our self-made, normal life and the thrill to be found only in God. As Paul expresses it in Romans 3:23, "For all have sinned and fallen short of the glory of God." Our sin splits off our relationship with God much as an iron wedge and an ax split birch wood. Falling short of His glory means that our sin keeps the thrill tantalizingly out of reach.

You'd be surprised by the types of sin that kill the thrill. Sure, the usual suspects are in the line-up: adultery, murder and the like. But some everyday problems are listed as sins too, like jealousy, anger, division, drunkenness, envy, disobedience to parents, lying, boasting and more (see Galatians 5:19 and Romans 1:30–31). The simple reality is that we've all sinned. Even if we think we've committed only "little" sins that are no big deal, the reality is that all sin, no matter how small, separates us from an authentic life of ecstasy in God.

We're split up, and we need help. To break free from this hellish lifestyle, we need a miracle. If we're honest, we know deep down that our entire bent is toward rebellion, pride, self-will and independence from God. No amount of effort on our part can break us free from slavery to sin (Romans 3:27–28). The truth is that we'll keep on missing the mark—no matter how hard we try.

We're just not as big on loving God as we are on loving ourselves. John Piper captures this truth like this: "All sin comes from not putting supreme value on the glory of God—this is the very essence of sin." Sin causes us to run hard—away from our end zone. It never allows us to witness the fist-pumping excitement of God. If we don't have God in our sights, cheering us on, we're running in the wrong direction.

We may seek *a* god, an idol, to make us feel better and to fill the vacuum in our hearts, but we'll get nowhere unless we're seeking the one true God, Who asks that we give up our self-centered ways to share our moments of victory with Him, just as I did that memorable evening with my dad. We can come to know that God. It all begins when we acknowledge the need to surrender our self-driven lives and admit our need for Jesus. Brokenness comes with the humbling realization that all parts of our lives are messed up and need God's help.

Desperation is our only route to salvation. People typically claim that desperate people are out of options. But in response there's mind-blowing, great news: If we're at the end of our rope and our ideas, slogging through a going nowhere, "normal" life, we're in the ideal position for God to show Himself strong. "For the foolishness of God is wiser than men, and the weakness of God is stronger than men" (1 Corinthians 1:25). Once we recognize our desperate need of God, we can begin moving toward the thrilling life He has planned for us.

KILL ME, GOD

The irony is that, if we want to live fully, something in us has to die. This means inviting God to put our self-will to death. It requires total surrender to God. We can't possibly experience the thrill and freedom of a life truly lived in God without first dying to our self (Romans 5:1–14). The most powerful and thrill-filled people have learned that if God doesn't kill us (the self-made, idolatrous us, that is), we have no chance of truly living.

The amazing thing about the freedom we can have in Jesus is that it's available only when we quit clinging to our own effort and give ourselves completely over to Him—a decision we make fresh every day. Some of the most profound insights about victory and thrill come from Watchman Nee in his book *The Normal Christian Life*:

"As long as we are trying to do anything, [God] can do nothing. It is because of our trying that we fail and fail and fail. God wants to demonstrate to us that we can do nothing at all, and until that is fully recognized our despair and disillusion will never cease." When we spend our lives "trying," we die a slow, agonizing death.

I've known the thrill of being alive in Christ, and I've also known the pain of returning to a self-directed life. I've attempted to look at outside factors and form a rationale for living in my own power by controlling, casting blame, demanding justice, desiring to be understood and explaining to God how screwed-up people really are. After arguing with God, there comes a point at which He responds "Are you done yet? I have so many great things to do in your life, but you have to let go and let me. Surrender your life, your twisted ways, even your deepest pain, and take a walk with Me into a new life beyond your wildest dreams!"

It's insanity to try to live the spiritual life in our own power. That was Paul's point when he wrote these powerful words in Galatians, words that are just as relevant today as they were then: "Let me ask you only this: Did you receive the Spirit by works of the law or by hearing with faith? Are you so foolish? Having begun by the Spirit, are you now being perfected by the flesh? Did you suffer so many things in vain—if indeed it was vain?" (Galatians 3:2-4). The thrill begins with acknowledging God and continues with complete dependence upon Him.

THINKING THRILL

The insanity plea actually works with God. He knows we live in a world that drives people to do crazy things. This lunacy revolves around one primary need: We're in search of thrill, and everyone is doing crazy things to find it. God has designed us to be wildly in need of stimulation, but even better, He's provided a way for us to find it. I've asked people, "Why did Jesus come to Earth?" Often they'll answer, "He's a great teacher, redeemer, and the ultimate sacrifice for our sins." These reasons, and many others like them, reveal the hard time we have grasping that God wants to care for our most primary need—to be restored to a joyful relationship with Him.

One of the central themes of this book is the following tweak of the Westminster Confession: *God is most glorified in us, as we are most satisfied in Him.* How can this be? Read this again slowly. *God is most glorified in us, as we are most satisfied in Him.* The reason we presume that authentic faith can't have anything to do with our joy is that we have a twisted perception of God. "Normal" people who live staunchly religious lives have crafted that false image. "Normalcy" actually places arduous demands on us: "Do more, give more, work harder, be nicer, and on and on...." This taskmaster view of God is false and keeps us alienated from the thrill.

"The insanity plea actually works with God. He knows we live in a world that drives people to do crazy things."

Remember the deadly deception I mentioned earlier? Jesus came up against similar lies during his time on Earth. He looked at the religious leaders and the honored teachers of His day and pronounced, "Woe to you, scribes and Pharisees, hypocrites! For you clean the outside of the cup and the plate, but inside they are full of greed and self-indulgence" (Matthew 23:25). The religious folk of Jesus' day thought they were good. Yet Jesus exposed them for the two-faced sinners they really were. Oh, they performed "acts of righteousness," but that was it. The operative word here is *acts!* As Jesus expressed it, they looked clean on the outside, but inside they were full of filth. It's like a stainless-steel travel mug that hasn't ever been washed on the inside.

The Pharisees claimed to have all the answers for life. They heaped tedious legalistic requirements onto their followers—requirements that went far beyond even the Jewish law—and hypocritically pronounced themselves to be holy. For them, it was all about control and about recruiting others to join them on the path of empty religion. They were actors who deserved Oscars. Jesus went so far as to call them thieves, killers and destroyers, proclaiming that He and only He offered the thrill of life.

It's time to start thinking *thrill!*

GOD-POWERED

Our "normal" Christian culture has one big, central problem. It's not the banning of prayer in our schools or a lack of self-effort. It's the presence of spiritual imitation and the lack of spiritual transformation. The greatest threat to thrill is trying to please God, all the while rejecting the power of God to transform our lives (2 Timothy 3:5). God is a champion of substance over style. Thrill is all about the raw, honest abandonment of our humanly devised rules and self-regulated lives. It's the humility to acknowledge that we can't bust free from the norm of normal apart from God's power.

God's thrill rejects the systems of pretense and points us to His mercy. It exposes acting and pretense as thrill killers. It causes us to desire the thrill of living authentically. Authentic living isn't easy, but it's the only solution for the pain of futile living in the land of Normal. People living genuinely know that nothing compares to the thrill found in trusting God.

I've been arrested twice. Once for a youthful misdemeanor while I was drunk. I kicked in a hotel room door and didn't pay for a night's sleep. I've never done that since. God also arrested me. He indicted me for living a normal life. But He also bailed me out. Since then, God has succeeded in transforming my whole life. I've never been the same since. And God continually invites me to lift my hands to Him, give up my life to His authority and tap into His power.

"God also arrested me. He indicted me For living a normal life. But He also bailed me out."

I've discovered that living in surrender is the best way to avoid the normal and to stay within the thrill. Surrender for me has brought with it the thrills of being an intentional dad, of increased intimacy with my bride, and of true friendship with people. I've something powerful to offer others through the intimate friendship I have with my Creator. God has altered every area of my life.

Good news for all you thrill seekers: God desires to do for you what He's done for me. Are you ready to surrender the normal life you've made for yourself? If so, this thrill's for you.

For personal or group study guides and leader support resources, go to www.ThrillOnline.net.

TWO

THRILL KILLER

**I steal innocence, kill by deception
and methodically destroy lives.**

— Thrill Killer

Shortly after the release of the movie *Schindler's List*, I went
to a late showing by myself. I'd heard the stories of view-
ers' emotional responses to the brutal and gut-wrenching
depiction of one of humanity's most heinous acts of evil —
the Holocaust — but nothing could have prepared me for
the depths of depravity I saw in that film. I witnessed a life-
altering story of unbearable grief, pain, torture, agony and
injustice. The emotional turmoil I felt impacts me to this
day. It was as though I had been right there, witnessing the
perpetrators stripping women and men naked and tearing
children from their mother's arms — right there but utterly
helpless to do anything. It was all I could do to contain my
hatred for this vile, systematic devastation of lives.

Commandant Amon Goeth took my emotions over the
top. The prison warden, Goeth was both a sexual deviant
and a psychotic killer. One particular scene involving Go-

eth ripped out my heart: Rising from his bed and leaving a mistress behind, he walks onto his balcony, cigarette in hand, bare-chested. Grabbing his rifle, he stares down the open sight, surveying hundreds of helpless Jews digging trenches and breaking rocks. They're unaware of Goeth's deadly disgust as he looks in boredom for any excuse to kill. As he scans the crowd, he notices a young, malnourished woman sitting by a wheelbarrow. Slowly putting down his cigarette, he takes aim and from a distance executes her without hesitation or remorse.

While the panicked prisoners work that much more frantically, Goeth's eyes roam for other targets who dare to pause for even a moment. As he nonchalantly surveys the prison yard, his bloodlust is momentarily satisfied. He stretches, his arms draped over the hot rifle lying across his bare shoulders, picks up his still-smoldering cigarette and strolls back inside.

Anger consumed me, seated there in the darkened theater, so much so that I could barely control my emotions. In that moment, if I could have killed Goeth, I would have.

DEADLY DECEPTION

Commandant Goeth was an outright killer, but the greatest threat to the Jews wasn't this open brutality but the vicious and carefully orchestrated deception of the Nazis. Hitler's regime was able to lure millions of Jews to their deaths with little or no organized resistance. The tactics of deception were documented in such firsthand testimonials as the diaries of Emanuel Ringelblum, who was executed in 1944.

Ringelblum addresses one of the most puzzling aspects of the Holocaust: How could so many millions of people have been passively led to their own destruction?

He records that, "In order to encourage people to volunteer for resettlement, the Nazis promised…that all those who voluntarily come to the transfer point for expulsion will receive three kilos of bread and a kilo of marmalade to take with them in their wanderings."

The Jews had been worn to the point of exhaustion by war and persecution. They were susceptible to deception because of their desire for survival. "Driven by hunger, anguish, a sense of hopelessness

> "…the greatest threat to the Jews wasn't this open brutality but the vicious and carefully orchestrated deception of the Nazis."

of their situation, [they] had not the strength to struggle any longer, simply had no place to live because they weren't assigned to any shop, and had no recourse but to go to their death voluntarily."

The deception continued right up to the bitter end. Ringelblum's description is graphic and sobering: "You may wonder why prisoners who had just gotten off the trains did not revolt, waiting as they did for hours (sometimes days!) to enter the gas chambers…. The Germans had perfected a diabolically clever and versatile system of collective death. In most cases the new arrivals did not know what awaited them. They were received with cold efficiency but without bestiality, invited to undress 'for the showers.' Sometimes they were handed soap and towels and were promised hot coffee after their showers. The gas chambers were, in fact, camouflaged as shower rooms, with pipes, faucets, dressing rooms, clothes hooks, and benches…."

IT'S NO MYTH

Deception hasn't only been used by evil men to bring about physical death; it's used by Thrill Killer to rob us of spiritual life. Maybe the most compelling evidence of his existence is that we either ignore him or associate him only with grotesque acts, ignoring his continuous attacks on our lives (Ephesians 6:10–12). He targets the young and the old, and his schemes go largely unnoticed. His influence seeps undetected into homes, hospitals, offices, schools and college campuses. He's a spiritual terrorist who can blend masterfully into any culture.

Thrill Killer's most effective weapons are intimidation and deception. Sometimes he acts like Goeth, surveying the courtyard of daily life and picking people off one-by-one, without warning. At other times he lures us into a lifeless existence through subtle deception. He wears us down, so that at our weakest moments we choose to believe what is false, wanting relief more than we want to face the truth.

How do we expose and disarm this stealthy enemy? Can we avoid becoming fatalities? How can we learn to spot the danger signs and escape the threat we face?

Spiritual warfare will always be a part of life on planet Earth, but we don't have to be casualties. There's hope for us. God wants to walk with us through deception and intimidation and to restore in us the passion for a thrilling life.

BORN FOR THRILL

One thing I know for certain: We're born for thrill. None of us comes into the world hoping for a mundane existence of boredom and mediocrity. Thrill Killer knows this too. And he's hell-bent on keeping us from discovering and enjoying our God-given birthright of a thrilling life.

I have a boyhood memory of my dad walking into the woods behind our house and shaking his head as he gazed high into the trees at the fort I was building. He just barked at me, "Please be careful." What a great dad.

A few months later the Alaskan winter set in. My friend and I piled up snow at the base of that tree house. We climbed high, even past the roof, where the limbs got thin. Then we did it: We free-fell into that snow pile, jumping up laughing and yelling,

"None of us comes into the world hoping for a mundane existence of boredom and mediocrity."

thrilled at the prospect of doing it again. It nearly gave my folks heart attacks, but, boy, was it a blast!

Think back to your own childhood. As kids, you weren't content to just sit and twiddle your thumbs! You wanted to explore the world, to experience new and exciting things. What happened to that child who saw beauty in worms and magic in catching a minnow three inches long? Some discovery-driven kids are fascinated by adventure. Scrapes and bruises come with the territory. Other kids create a pretend family with dolls — dressing, feeding, talking, singing lullabies and tucking them in for bedtime. Still others toss a baseball for hours, imagining they're in the big leagues and vicariously hearing the crowds roar.

Kids love to run around like crazy and yell at the top of their lungs, or ride bikes as fast as they can down gravel roads. Some ski black diamond runs, while others are just as excited when they gather the courage to swim in the deep end of the pool. As kids, we lived on the edge. Each of us wanted to live life for the sheer thrill of it.

CHEAP COUNTERFEITS

God has created us all to be natural-born thrill seekers. But there's a problem. Somewhere along the way, as we got older, we diluted thrill's definition and lost our vision for the real thing. We became respectable and mature. But as we grew up our passion chilled. We started thinking in terms of safety instead of adventure. The caveat "but" began to litter our sentences. We started to say things like "That sounds awesome. It could be great, *but* it also sounds dangerous and risky," or "I've always wanted to do that, *but* I'm afraid to try it," or "I'm ready to change, *but* I'm afraid this is the way things will always be."

> "Instead of our spiritual Father having to caution "Just be careful," He's asking "Why are you playing it so safe?"

Slowly, unwittingly, we've allowed the thrill to disappear from our lives. We've given someone or something else the authority to kill our excitement, to trap us in normal, dull, respectable lives. We've begun to think in terms of how others view us instead of how God sees us. This approach to life blocks us off from the thrill God has designed us to enjoy. Instead of our spiritual Father having to caution "Just be careful," He's asking "Why are you playing it so safe?"

Some of us try to quench the desire for thrill God has placed within us with counterfeits. We have a God-shaped vacuum in our hearts that we try to fill with anything we think will make us feel good, look better or become more powerful. Some of us may define thrill in terms of violence, drug and alcohol abuse, and sexual addictions. Others settle for less damaging ways to fill the void and ease the nagging pain. We spend our nights glued to the TV or surfing the Internet. We spend money we don't have on things we don't need. We overeat and numb our feelings with things that leave us empty. We do all these things to assuage our need for that now-elusive thrill. But nothing works. We often hurt others by doing things we never before could have imagined doing—stealing their thrill while trying to achieve our own.

EXPOSING A KILLER

As we've seen in *Schindler's List*, Commandant Goeth is the consummate killer—smart, greedy for power and money, ambitious and so sick with evil that death is his delight. Depriving others of life is the way he medicates his own madness. Others' pain equates to his own pleasure. He epitomizes the Nazis' desire for Arian supremacy and world domination, committing unspeakable atrocities, untroubled by conscience.

Goeth is a flesh-and-blood image of Thrill Killer, who hates us and craves nothing more than our spiritual death. He wants to suck the thrill out of life and keep us separated from the passionate love God has for us (see Genesis 3:1–5). Since the dawn of humanity, Thrill Killer has been slaying the young and the old, the rich and the poor, the strong and the weak—and he's still picking off people today. He plays dirty—tempting, accusing, ridiculing and mocking us. He hits us when we're up and crushes us when we're down. He has laid millions to waste by keeping them from an authentic relationship with God through Jesus Christ.

Thrill Killer finds his joy when our excitement with God is either never realized or is quickly stolen away. He loves to make free people think they're captives. He's a master at twisting truth into a lie.

Thrill Killer must be exposed. We need to know the vicious lies he's spreading through twisted words, religious busyness, false guilt and unwarranted shame. None of us is immune to his attacks. We're all targets.

NORMAL IS NOT ENOUGH

We've been imprisoned for so long that we've come to the point of reasoning that normal *is* enough, that the thrill of spiritual liberty is for a select few—that it's reserved for pastors or "super-Christians." And Thrill Killer uses this lie to keep us confined to a state of spiritual apathy—fully accepting of a "moderated religion." In a very real sense, we're in a spiritual concentration camp, getting picked off one at a time.

> "In a very real sense, we are in a spiritual concentration camp, getting picked off one at a time."

Thrill Killer doesn't expose himself in the open. He can disguise himself as the voice of reason and spout vicious lies about God. He tells us that God isn't good, that God is demanding, and that God can't deliver real thrill. Thrill Killer convinces us that we're on our own, that the best we can hope for is the status quo.

Thrill Killer wants us to believe that we deserve and should expect only what's "normal." Status quo is where the majority of the world lives. He mocks passion for God. Thrill Killer invites us to be led by the majority. He wants us to ask ourselves "Who am I to think I can have more than most?"

Thrill Killer is fanatical about silencing the voice of God. He wants us to hear everyone else's voices: our bosses, our critics, our spouses—and sometimes even our pastors, as a substitute for listening to God. He fears God's voice and the excitement it builds in us. Deep down we want to believe that *normal isn't enough*. We want to hope that God has so much more for us. We want to experience the thrill-filled life. But, as Jesus warns us in John 10:10, "The thief comes only to steal and kill and destroy." The thief can show up as a false teacher, as a boatload of poisonous words from families or spiritual bullies, or as any other toxic waste dumped into our minds and souls. He'll do anything to keep us from believing that God has a supernatural plan for us to live out. But the thief isn't going to have the last word. Jesus goes on in John 10:10 to declare, "I came that they may have life and have it abundantly."

Yes, thrilling life! How awesome is that? Do we want this life? Do we want the peace and power of God? How about the love, patience, self-control and joy of God? Unraveling Thrill Killer's lies leads to liberation. Jesus wants His truth to free us from captivity. When we're in Christ, Thrill Killer becomes a powerless enemy.

RANSOMED!

As much as *Schindler's List* is a depiction of the ugliness of human nature, it's also a story of redemption. The story line revolves around two contrasting themes—Amon Goeth's vile desire to exterminate Jews and Oskar Schindler's tireless efforts to save as many of them as possible from Goeth's Kraków-Plaszów concentration camp.

Far from being a faultless man, Schindler was a materialist and a womanizer. He looked for satisfaction in the "stuff" of life and built his fortune by ingenuity and manipulation. But as Nazi brutality against the Jews became more and more blatant, Schindler's heart changed. He became less concerned with making money, so much so that he began to perceive that his greed had blinded him to the anguish all around him. Deciding to save as many Jews as he possibly could — no matter the cost — he concocted a plan to purchase his former employees and their families. Not for personal gain but simply to save the people he knew and had begun to love.

At the end of the movie, Schindler has to flee the approaching Red Army, leaving behind the Jews he has ransomed to be liberated by the Soviets. He ends up penniless, having spent everything to purchase freedom for as many workers as possible. Before he departs, the Jews he has saved from Goeth's destruction give him a gift: a ring fashioned from gold extracted from their teeth. It's the only thing of value they could think to offer their rescuer. On the ring is inscribed this phrase: "Whoever saves one life saves the entire world."

In brokenness and tears, Schindler laments to his Jewish friend that he didn't do enough. He should have saved more people from such horrific death. By the end of the movie, Schindler has changed from a greedy, disconnected employer of Jewish laborers to a man who has poured all he had into saving the lives of those he had formerly employed. All told, Schindler rescued over a thousand Jewish men, women and children from the gas chambers of Auschwitz.

The Jews on Schindler's list knew they couldn't save themselves. They were scheduled for extermination. Their only hope was to be ransomed — bought with a price. And a high price it was. Oskar Schindler willingly gave all he had. He spent his entire fortune on the bribes Goeth demanded for each worker. Schindler purchased their right to live by paying the price they could not.

Many of us are trapped in a spiritual concentration camp. We've come to expect a life without thrill. We're occupied with joyless busyness. At times, we hurt deeply and hunger for something to fill us up inside. We have nowhere to run, and many of us feel alone even among friends and family. We ignore our pain and just try to get by. Our addictions, sins and hurts have built walls around our souls. We long to be set free!

I have some awesome news for you! Just as the Jews on Schindler's list were bought with a price—literally ransomed from death—Jesus Christ was willing to pay the price to save us: "This is good, and it is pleasing in the sight of God our Savior, who desires all people to be saved and to come to the knowledge of the truth. For there is one God, and there is one mediator between God and men, the man Christ Jesus, who gave himself as a *ransom* for all, which is the testimony given at the proper time" (1 Timothy 2:3-6, emphasis mine). But this rescue isn't just salvation from death; it's the freedom to experience a brand new life—a life of thrill.

FREEDOM FIGHTERS

It's fair to say that I'm a Jesus follower and a freedom fighter. The battle we're facing is in identifying Thrill Killer's tactics and fighting for liberation—freedom from all the chains and garbage that hold people back from a thrilling life. It's about Jesus Christ, our redeemer and ransom from Thrill Killer's concentration camp.

Even if you already call yourself a Christian. Real Thrill goes way beyond "accepting" Christ because many Christians live far removed from God's thrill-filled vision for us.

If you think that because I wrote this book I'm some kind of spiritual professional who's got it all figured out, you couldn't be further from the truth. Comparison is one of the tools Thrill Killer uses to defeat us. The reality is that I'm just like many of you. In fact, before Jesus set me free,

I was a complete mess. I've experienced desperate nights strung out on cocaine, gripped by fear and loneliness, filled with despair. I've had moments when I lost all hope. I know the shame of crash-and-burn failure. I've run from God and gone my own way.

"If you think that because I wrote this book I'm some kind of spiritual professional who's got it all figured out, you couldn't be further from the truth."

I want you to understand something. If you get nothing else from this book, get this: It wasn't God's intention for me to live a thrill-less life. And it isn't His intention for you, either, to live in defeat.

I know that some who have been ransomed by God have returned to their old place of captivity. Thrill Killer has them living as though they had never been set free. This has happened to me at times because of outright lies, subtle deception and simple lack of attention to truth. But Jesus wants to set us free again, to walk with us and to protect us from Thrill Killer's tactics.

God, by His great mercy and love, rescued me from hell, both here on Earth and in the life to come. He drew me to Himself in kindness and saved me through Jesus' death and resurrection. I'm so thankful that He's alive and that I, in turn, am alive in Him. Jesus had my name on His list, and He gave everything He had—including His very life—to ransom me. And He's promised never to leave me. He's still helping me guard my freedom. And He'll do the same for you, if you let Him.

THIS THRILL'S FOR YOU

Every chapter in this book will continue to expose another of Thrill Killer's lies. No doubt you'll recognize at least some of them in your life. I know I have. But I want you to keep in the forefront of your mind that while Thrill Killer's lies are potent, God's truth can expose and thwart them. God is the Great Liberator. He's the only one able not only to save us from Thrill Killer but to fill us with unspeakable joy.

We're not meant to settle for the boring and the mundane. We've been ransomed, redeemed and set free. We're invited by God's kindness to walk with Jesus and to experience true fulfillment. We're destined to know the deep love and joy that come from living fully in God.

Normal isn't enough. This thrill's for you!

For personal or group study guides and leader support resources, go to www.ThrillOnline.net.

THREE
LET'S DANCE

I want Christ's followers to be sophisticated, segregated and dull.

—Thrill Killer

My kids love to remind me what a strange dad I am. I admit I've done some bizarre things. One of the more embarrassing memory lanes they like to take me down involves our spontaneous "Let's Dance" celebrations. This is the way it worked. We'd be driving down a road, through a parking lot, or in line at a drive-thru when the urge would hit me, and boom! I'd crank up the stereo, whip open the door, get out and dance so vigorously I'd come close to injury. I'm sure it wasn't pretty. When the kids were little they'd jump out with me and try to outdo dad. We'd jump back into the car laughing our heads off, and anyone who'd seen us usually wore a bewildered look. As the kids got older they stayed in the car and hid. Then a sad day came when they looked at me as though I were in the principal's office and said "Dad, you can't do this anymore." I was embarrassed because it finally hit me just how odd "Let's Dance" really was.

> **"'Dad, you can't do this anymore.' I was embarrassed because it finally hit me just how odd 'Let's Dance' really was."**

As passionate as I am, I resisted for years my desire to express my love for God. I battled fears of what people would think if I exposed my excitement about God. Even when sharing the story of my life change, I resisted opening up about how dramatically God had changed me and about my big-time love for Him. I'm not talking about being crazy, weird or culturally odd but about giving genuine expression to all that I know and feel to be true about Him.

Thrill Killer wants to keep a lid on our celebration of God, whether it's in a church service, talking with someone at the office or sharing with our families in the privacy of our homes. Thrill Killer doesn't mind if our worship is dull. On the other hand, he isn't concerned if we're so extreme that people conclude we've lost our minds (check out 1 Corinthians 14:23).

Thrill Killer is an expert in cultural division. He has mastered the arts of sophistication, segregation and dullness. If he can keep different groups from enjoying worship together and learning from each other, he pulls off a victory. We begin to see Scripture through lenses of cultural experience and personal preference.

Does our response to God really matter? Can authentic worship impact the world around us? Does it make any difference to God? Is there personal benefit to being stretched by people from various cultural backgrounds? The answer to each of these questions is a rock-solid yes!

Yes, there is a reason to dance.

FIT FOR A KING

You couldn't accuse Israel's King David of lacking passion. Do a quick read of David's writings in the Psalms, and you'll find the full range of human emotions on display over the course of his adventurous life. He was a child-warrior who killed wild animals to protect his flocks, a designated king who lived on the run from his best friend's dad, and a legendary general who led amazing military campaigns. And all this before he reached 30, when he finally became king. The Bible tells us that David accomplished these feats because "the LORD, the God of hosts, was with him" (2 Samuel 5:10).

One story in particular gives a crystal clear picture of David's unbridled passion for God. The ark of the covenant, Israel's holiest object, was finally being carried back to Jerusalem. Shortly after David became king, he had gathered 30,000 of Israel's best warriors to escort the ark back home. Because the ark was God's earthly throne in the Old Testament, it symbolized the very power of God. The prospect of having God's power back in Jerusalem filled David with joy. And we're not talking miniscule pleasure. As the ark entered the city, "David danced before the LORD with all his might" (2 Samuel 6:14). David dancing with all his might must have been something to see. He'd displayed some serious strength in the past, so you know this was no shuffling.

This display didn't set well with his wife, Michal. Watching covertly from a window, she spied him "leaping and dancing before the LORD." The Bible tells us that in her heart she "despised him." Later, after his celebration, she scolded him: "'How the king of Israel dishonored himself today, uncovering himself today before the eyes of his servants' female servants, as one of the vulgar fellows shamelessly uncovers himself!'"

David's reply: "It was before the LORD, who chose me above your father and above all his house, to appoint me as prince over Israel, the people of the LORD—and I will make merry before the LORD" (2 Samuel 6:20–21).

This was a worship war. David freely worshiped God with everything in himself, while Michal despised him for it and sought to kill his thrill. Thrill Killer knows the threat of God-honoring worship, and he'll do anything and use anyone to destroy it.

"Worship wars still happen today. The desire to genuinely express personal gratitude to God is often squelched by fear of rejection."

Worship wars still happen today. The desire to genuinely express personal gratitude to God is often squelched by fear of rejection. Some people are afraid that others will think they're too excited about God. Others fear they might be judged for not being excited enough. Either way, the result is loss of authentic interaction with God. Losing the capacity to worship subtly impacts the world in a real way. What some see as their responsibility to be measured and "not get too excited" can be a thin veil for their own doubts, fear or need for image management.

DANGEROUS SWING

When God transformed my life, I slid over into some dangerous territory. I became what I now call an *angry evangelical*. While I loved God and had a passion for people to meet Him, I had quickly built a box around God. In fact, I think it's safe to say that while I was trying to please the Holy One by following rules, the evil one was chuckling as I turned into a joyless legalist, sucking life out of those around me.

A position of power is bad for any legalist. In my first year at Multnomah University, I ran for student body president and won. When it came time to take office, I was ready. I had an agenda, and no one was going to get in my way! I was the kind of president you either loved or hated, and I was convinced that those who hated me were out of touch with God.

One day, the class secretary showed me a couple of unsigned letters written to me by people pointing out my legalist tendencies. They were probably accurate, but they weren't kind. We took those letters, put them on a corkboard and threw darts at them. Not a healthy response, I know. I wasn't being malicious, but in some areas my passion had created spiritual blindness. My zeal was both contagious and dangerous. I wanted to make a difference, and much of what our student cabinet achieved that year was positive, but we also hurt people by failing to show them the basic courtesy of good manners — much less the love of God.

GOD IN A BOX

I was a buttoned-down legalist. You know the kind: a keeper of a long "no" list and short "yes" list: no drinking, no smoking, no dancing, no cussing. Because God had saved me from so much bad stuff, I swung the pendulum way over to the other side — which might have been worse! I was a walking contradiction.

The most conspicuous act in my Hall of Shame as Multnomah University student body president was helping lead a student protest against graduation because I didn't approve of the worship style of the church in which the ceremony was being held. Its members raised their hands, exercised spiritual gifts for which I had no tolerance, and had a reputation for getting a little wild during their services. The box I constructed for God had no place for this style of worship. I went toe-to-toe with the administration and held meetings to formulate a response. Because of my influence, some seniors refused to walk for their diplomas.

Later on I realized the damage caused by my actions, but it was too late. I was a willing participant in Thrill Killer's plan to divide believers based on my view of what correct worship looked like. I was a passionate zealot who needed God to fill my heart and mind with His desire to draw people together, not divide them. The truth is that I screwed up when I tried to put God in a box. That box actually ended up imprisoning me.

The danger with pigeon-holing God is that we can miss Him when He's standing right in front of us. Some spiritual leaders during Jesus' time were so determined to live by their personal definition of godliness that they completely missed God. They missed out on supernatural healings taking place right before their eyes (Luke 13:10–17). They even missed out on the joy of seeing God transform sinners because their box had no room for mercy (see Matthew 9:9–13). Forcing God into a manmade box is not only short-sighted but deadly.

BREAKING FREE

It took two years for God to finish a grueling work in my heart and to convince me to break free of my prison of legalism. He knew what it would take to rip out my legalistic heart, make it tender and put it back so it could beat in synch with His.

While I was living in South Africa and coaching a track team, God blew through me in a fresh way one early morning. A great preacher, Charles Swindoll, had written a book titled *The Grace Awakening*. As I sat reading that book at 3 a.m., God smoked me with this quote: "You want to mess up the minds of your children? Here's how—guaranteed! Rear them in a legalistic tight context of external religion, where performance is more important than reality.... Embrace a long list of do's and don'ts publicly, but hypocritically practice them privately, yet never own up to the fact that it's hypocrisy. Act one way and live another. And you can count on it—emotional and spiritual damage will occur." I had an awesome two-year old son and newborn daughter, and I never wanted to be that kind of dad to them.

After reading a bit more, I wept for hours, asking God to forgive my pathetic attitude and misguided passion. He heard my prayers. And it was as though God opened the floodgates. His love and Spirit filled me in a fresh way. I stepped into another dimension of freedom in every area of my life—including that of being a dad. The next morning I called the president of Multnomah, Dr. Joe Aldrich. I informed him that I recognized my legalism and judgmental spirit and asked for his forgiveness. He was gracious, telling me, "I know you love God deeply, Karl, and that He would work these attitudes out of you in time." Thank God for gracious Christ-followers like Dr. Aldrich.

> **"You want to mess up the minds of your children? Here's how—guaranteed! Rear them in a legalistic tight context of external religion."**

FREEDOM CALLING

Putting other people in boxes is destructive too. Today I see everything very differently. When God awakened me and shook up my unloving view of others, He set me on a path of freedom. He didn't just set me free from legalism; He set me free to worship Him with the truth of His Word as my guide. God's definition of freedom is *huge*. He has a unique call for everyone—and that's a life-changing realization. We're on God's dance floor, and it's a big one where everyone is welcome.

The reality is that I wasn't the only legalist around—there are many more still in bondage. Rule-oriented people who segregate believers unknowingly help Thrill Killer in his quest to discredit God. In their zeal for religion, they exclude people and worship styles that are different from their own. Without knowing it, they're selling Thrill Killer's lie, insisting that "God only wants one style of worship." They see God's kingdom as one of exclusion and fail to recognize God as loving and inclusive. Jesus never created divisions around cultural or socioeconomic differences.

The Gospels demonstrate throughout that Jesus had a radically loving view of the way God relates to the world. His entire life displayed God's character. From the beginning Jesus defied the status quo and challenged all cultural and religious conventions. No story reflects this better than His encounter with the woman at the well.

DIVINE APPOINTMENT

One day, after a long and tiring trek, Jesus sat down at a well and spoke about worship with a woman who had a reputation for sleeping around. In that culture, a Jewish man would never have sat down with a Samaritan (they were called "dogs" by the Jews because they had inbred with their captors in earlier times). In fact, most Jewish men would've walked around the whole territory of Samaria on their way to Jerusalem, not through it. And rabbis certainly didn't sit down and discuss worship with loose women— or even, for that matter, with women in general. Yet Jesus purposefully walked through Samaria and intentionally engaged the adulterous woman at the well. Talk about shredding the status quo!

Jesus knew her outcast status. She came to the well at high noon, the hottest part of the day, because no one else would have been there at that time. She didn't want to deal with the shame of their harsh words and mockery. Her life was spent hiding from the gossip of "decent" people, trying to gain security from simultaneous relations with several men, and coping with her rejection. As she approached the well, she too must have been hot and weary. All she wanted was to fill her jug and get back home without any hassle.

> "Her life was spent hiding from the gossip of 'decent' people, trying to gain security from simultaneous relations with several men, and coping with her rejection."

Yet here sat a Jewish man asking her for a drink. He wasn't supposed to talk to her, much less ask her for water. Imagine how she must have felt at that moment. This encounter was probably the last thing she wanted. But when Jesus mentioned living water in contrast to well water, He piqued her interest. What did she have to lose? She asked for His living water.

Jesus knew her true needs and with one statement gently exposed her private shame: "Jesus said to her, 'Go, call your husband, and come here.' The woman answered him, 'I have no husband.' Jesus said to her, 'You are right in saying, "I have no husband"; for you have had five husbands, and the one you now have is not your husband. What you have said is true'" (John 4:16-18). He agreed and affirmed her for voicing the ugly truth about her lifestyle.

From the fact that Jesus had inside information about her, the woman correctly concluded that He had a pipeline to God. And this insight opened her mind and heart to what He had to teach her—that the Father seeks "true worshipers" who worship in spirit *and* in truth. Seeking clarification, she asked, "'Sir, I perceive that you are a prophet. Our fathers worshiped on this mountain, but you say that in Jerusalem is the place where people ought to worship.' Jesus said to her, 'Woman, believe me, the hour is coming when neither on this mountain nor in Jerusalem will you worship the Father'" (John 4:19-21). Jesus had already broken cultural taboos by walking through Samaria and by speaking to a Samaritan—and an adulterous woman to boot! Now He was breaking religious taboos as well!

CRUSHING BARRIERS

With this statement, Jesus struck a decisive blow against ethnic barriers. He saw a cultural wall that needed to be smashed. In His day, as in our own, race was a major cause of division, pain and anger. As a matter of fact, segregation has been around since the dawn of history. The long-term wounds inflicted by racism and segregation are painful signs pointing to a need for God's intervention. Both the victims and the perpetrators of segregation need the radical truth of the Gospel to heal them.

Jesus, the sinless man, knew what it's like to be hated by the powerful. He was falsely tried and convicted, beaten by soldiers who flailed His skin, and executed on a cross, even though He had done nothing wrong. Ever since the days of his earthly ministry, Jesus has been toppling the barriers of race and class, dismantling social and religious segregation.

All kinds of issues can erect barriers between people. Jesus is all about tearing them down. When He sat at a well and signaled that there's no place for racism in the worship of God, His intention wasn't only to care for the needs of this woman in pain but also to invite the Samaritans onto the dance floor of worship.

> "When anyone steps onto the dance floor of worship, his or her voice and unique dance moves are acceptable to the Creator."

Here's a powerful truth: *Every human being is equally worthy of God's attention.* As Paul writes to the Galatians, "There is neither Jew nor Greek, there is neither slave nor free, there is neither male nor female, for you are all one in Christ Jesus" (Galatians 3:28). When anyone steps onto the dance floor of worship, his or her voice and unique dance moves are acceptable to the Creator. When Jesus stated that worship would not be regulated by geography, He was declaring that the day of considering the Samaritans — and all Gentiles, for that matter — as lower than the Jews was over. All are coequal children of God.

ONE RACE—THE HUMAN RACE

We can't possibly know God if we don't know Jesus, and Jesus loved all people equally. And we're alike members of one race — the human race!

Let's be clear. God isn't exclusionary; He's *inclusive*. Jesus let His hatred of segregation be known. No doubt he would have been sitting with Rosa Parks that memorable day on the bus. He would have stood staunchly against racism while being water-cannoned in Arkansas. He would have led any opposition to the Nazis and protested the policy of apartheid in South Africa. He desires to scrub our souls and minds clean of any racism and cultural pride that separates us from each other, and then to replace it with His radical love for all humanity. If we, as Christ-followers, want to glorify our great God, our churches must reflect the cultural diversity of our cities. And not just culture diversity, but class diversity as well. The era of the cookie-cutter Christian must come to an end. Diversity is everywhere: in schools, in workplaces and in families. Well, almost everywhere; it isn't evident in many churches, even though God wants all people everywhere to worship Him in unity.

For many years I've entertained a passion for seeing diversity in church services. During my nine years as a pastor in Anchorage, I saw God transform hundreds of lives. The growth was significant and sustained. My particular desire was to see God increase the mix of families from Alaska's native, Asian, Hispanic and Island-nation cultures in the church. The dream was to celebrate together in an all-inclusive manner, embracing the beauty of the music, teaching and worship style of each group to the one true God. I knew two things for sure: Like Jesus, we needed to go out of our way to make this happen, and we couldn't just talk about it. We prayed for God to show us how to act. And He did.

It took courage for several individuals and families to step into leadership. They were clearly in the minority, but they didn't flinch as they served and helped lead our church. And something explosive happened. The church grew rapidly in size, and ethnic diversity was dramatically increased. We were never to be the same again.

SPIRIT *AND* TRUTH

One of the realities involved with God calling everyone to worship Him is that people of different backgrounds and cultures will do so in different ways. Some churches encourage quiet reverence rather than exuberance. Others promote louder music, with lots of instruments, versus the strains of solemn pipe organs filling the sanctuary. Some prefer rock bands or soloists singing contemporary music instead of hymns. Traditions and upbringing shape our preferred style more than any other factors. Sometimes this creates tension among Christ-followers.

I've had the privilege of joining the solemn worship at a small hermitage in northwest Arkansas, complete with candles and meditation. I've also stood among tens of thousands of Zulu's in KwaMashu township, South Africa, raucously praising God as though we were bringing in a new year. When it came to worship, Jesus was a champion of authenticity over any set style. Keeping it real was paramount for the Savior of the world. That's why He told the Samaritan woman essentially that "true worshipers will worship the Father in spirit and truth, for the Father is seeking such people to worship him" (John 4:22–24; paraphrase mine).

Did you get that? God is seeking authentic worshipers, and Jesus described genuine worship as an expression of spirit *and* truth.

EPOXY WORSHIP

I used to work with my dad in the garage. The fix-up king, he taught me a lot about home building and repairs. One of Dad's favorite glues was epoxy. Epoxy works on a simple principle: *Mix part A with part B, and you get glue.* If you don't mix it together, epoxy won't work. Part A can't do the job alone, and Part B has no strength on its own.

I find epoxy to be a useful metaphor for worship. Worship works only when it involves a mixture of spirit and truth. People who worship in spirit alone lack sufficient grounding in the Scriptures and the knowledge of God. Others, who worship only in truth, stifle the emotional response that exudes from us when God is working in our lives. The answer to this division is simple but powerful: We need to bring together all that we know to be true about God *and* all the emotion we feel toward Him. Using our unique, God-given personalities in combination with God's truth permeating our minds makes for worship that connects with the heart of God.

> **"We need to bring together all that we know to be true about God *and* all the emotion we feel toward Him."**

WORSHIP: PART A

Sports are a big part of our cultural expression. In fact, I'd venture to say that for many people participating in or witnessing sporting events is on par with a worship experience. I too love watching sports, and almost any event will do. But there are certain games about which I'm particularly passionate. For instance, if I'm watching a team on which I know someone, or if that team is *my* team, I'm going to cheer a lot harder than for a game that features teams I neither know nor care about.

I'm by nature a demonstrative guy, so my cheering at times gets pretty wild. I have no inhibitions against hopping up and down, yelling, hootin' and hollering. And don't even get me started on the refs! When I'm really into a game, other spectators must look at me and wonder "What's this guy on?" Perhaps you're the same way about your passions. Now here's the thing about passion: It never manifests itself passively. If you're zealous about something, people can tell by the way you speak about, cheer for and promote it.

Don't get thrown off here. Passion doesn't necessarily require shouting, clapping and fist pumping. Here's the point, though: *The better we know God and the more we connect with Him, the more authentic, passionate and active our worship should be!* And how that looks to others shouldn't really matter.

Our worship of God should be as real as our cheering at sporting events, our tears at the births of our children, our applause at graduations, and more. I'm a man who pumps my fists in the air and cheers at close games. I do the same now in the worship of my God because this is my way of being true to what I know and how I feel. Still, at other times I feel the need just to contemplate and listen, because I do that in life too. Life isn't always a celebration. We may experience pain over the loss of a family member, a close friend, a job or a relationship. In such times, contemplative worship becomes a venue for healing and comfort. Whether our worship is boisterous or somber, the point is that authentic worship is always done in spirit *and* in truth.

WORSHIP: PART B

We need a healthy dose of truth to accompany our emotion. Bringing truth to our minds balances our soul like ballast in a boat and enhances the emotions of worshiping God. Our mind is the control center that directs our lives. What we put in it on a steady basis is critical for spiritual survival and worship. Jesus said, "If you abide in my word, you are truly my disciples, and you know the truth, and the truth will set you free" (John 8:31–32). The freedom that God holds out to us is real. Our minds need regular deposits of truth in order to sustain clear thinking, freedom and authentic worship.

I recently helped my son's friend. He's a new Christ-follower, and Thrill Killer was hammering him. I pointed him to Romans 8:18–39. This chunk of truth is tremendous for anyone under the weight of accusation and discouragement. Beside himself with excitement, he called me after spending time reading these verses: "Verse 28 really encouraged me. It tells me that all my embarrassing junk and the mess I've made of my life aren't wasted." That verse reads, "And we know that for those who love God all things work together for good, for those who are called according to his purpose." My son's friend went on to say, "It's so cool that God can do this for me." He was grateful for truthful words describing God's love and promises. God's truth ignited authentic worship in this young man. There's inexhaustible truth in the Bible, and it leads to inexhaustible worship.

HONEST TO GOD

Worship isn't a weird thing. It's the most common activity in the world. In fact, it's part of what makes us human. Worship is the response of people to those things in which they find life. As we've seen in his response to his wife, David teaches us something very important about worship: The style of worship isn't the issue. The object of worship is. David worshiped for an audience of one—God. When our ultimate affection is focused on God alone, we can state with David, "I will celebrate before the LORD."

These are the words of a man who was completely authentic. "A man after God's heart," as the Bible describes David. Even Michal's attempt to shame David is met with a simple response: "I will be held in honor."

"Worship is the response of people to those things in which they find life."

David understood that as we honor God before men, we'll also be honored before our Father in heaven. As Jesus says, "So everyone who acknowledges me before men, I also will acknowledge before my Father who is in heaven" (Matthew 10:32). When we acknowledge and acclaim God, we won't be intimidated or distracted by trivial fights over how to worship Him. The big picture lesson from David's dance story is to be true to the joy God brings us. He is our defender and friend, and He loves our responses to Him.

I love world cup soccer. One aspect that grabs me is the passionate, crazy, noisy fans. Amazing! The chanting, singing and flag-waving pulsate throughout the broadcast. Those fans really know how to celebrate. Their intensity is all about their country pride, and when there's a score... oh, baby!

I wonder what would happen if God's children got a little more excited about Him. I'm not talking about losing our minds and rioting but about fired-up noise for God that demonstrates heartfelt passion for His kingdom! Too many of God's kids are stuck in the wilderness of long-faced solemnity. We need to become fully engaged worshipers of God! After all, this is how God responds when we turn to Him. Remember the story of the prodigal son? The father ran to his returning son, threw his arms around him and then threw a huge party for him. It's a picture of how God celebrates us when we approach Him. We need to consider ourselves *privileged* to demonstrate our gratitude in return. No, I'm not suggesting disrespect toward our heavenly Father. Or avoidance of the realities of a painful world. Sometimes it makes the best sense to kneel or cry during worship. We emotionally celebrate or mourn life's varied experiences; why wouldn't this be reflected in the ways in which we relate to our Creator?

GET ON THE DANCE FLOOR

A moderated religion will never truly display the unbelievable glory and greatness of our God. Who in the world would want to join half-hearted, hands-in-the-pockets people who are staunchly committed to avoiding excitement? I've witnessed the manner in which contagious, authentic worship can transform hearts. On more than one occasion I've witnessed people coming into a celebration of authentically worshiping people and having their hearts powerfully touched by God. When lost and spiritually empty people witness a fully integrated church worshiping in spirit and truth, they can't ignore the implications. They're compelled to come to grips with the God who is the source of such joy.

Some of you have repressed your God-given desire to pour out your hearts to Him in loving, emotional response to His grace. You've bought into a lie about God, convinced that He expects somber and stifled worship. You've been cautioned that excitement and emotional outbursts may dishonor God. Nothing could be further from the truth. God loves you the exact way He designed you—emotions included!

The reality is that we're all worshipers. We're all passionate about something. We're all emotionally connected to people and things in life. Thrill Killer is trying to steal away one of the most natural, normal (in the best possible way) and thrilling expressions of the human spirit. If we worship the things God has created for our enjoyment instead of the Creator Himself, Thrill Killer has once again succeeded. Our full range of emotions, passions and personality should be part of our worship of our great God.

Having read this chapter, you may feel that the notion of being this thrilled about God, while enticing, is at best a remote possibility for you. Here's the tough news: Some of you are under deep spiritual deception. The thrill seems elusive because your soul is detached from God. But here comes the good news: True faith can be yours today. The following chapters will liberate your soul and take you on a journey that will cause even the most mellow among you to dance.

Like all relationships, adjustments take time and focus. The reality is that true worship requires simple choices. Begin by forgetting about what others think and choosing to direct your worship to God, for His eyes only. You're a child of God, redeemed by Jesus, saved from your sins and loved beyond all imagination—so *rejoice*! God is thrilled about you, and you can find your thrill in worshiping Him in spirit and in truth. God celebrates you! Now, that's a reason to dance!

For personal or group study guides and leader support resources, go to www.ThrillOnline.net.

FOUR

BIG HOLY AUDACIOUS GOD

**I want people to believe that God is puny,
out of touch and impotent.**

—Thrill Killer

In 1991 my young family had just returned to the U.S. after a year in South Africa. While there, I'd coached a track team, our daughter had been born, and we'd seen God do some amazing things in a township negatively affected by apartheid. Life had been an adventure every day. Getting back to the U.S. seemed a whole lot more "normal."

Upon moving to Denver, where I could continue my biblical training, I started a little business to get us on our feet. The business was taking off, and we bought some rigs. My pickup had that new-truck smell. As I pulled into the driveway, my family ran outside, bursting with excitement. I told my bride we were going out for burgers to celebrate. Turns out we were in for a whole lot more.

CITIZEN'S ARREST

As we headed down Colorado Boulevard, we noticed something unusual. A car was weaving through traffic—in the wrong direction—bouncing off cars left and right. I was pretty sure this out-of-control driver was drunk, and he was heading straight for us! At the last second, the driver sobered up enough to realize he was on the wrong side of the median. He turned through an intersection and headed down the correct side of the road, leaving behind a trail of damaged cars and irate people.

Well, I couldn't have that!

I warned my family to hold on, and in my brand new truck I took a sharp left, hit the curb hard, popped the front wheels off the ground, and jumped the median. The chase was on!

I pulled into the three-lane road filled with traffic and waited at a red light. The drunk driver was at the front of the line, thankfully aware enough to stop at the red light. Rolling down our windows, we yelled to the guys on our right and left about what was going on and asked for their help in stopping this guy. They were both with me, and when the light turned green we were off.

The three of us wound through traffic and got behind the drunk driver. He tried to turn onto the Interstate, but I shot around him on the shoulder and spun my truck sideways to block the entrance. He veered back onto Colorado Boulevard and headed for the overpass. One of my new comrades got in front of him, the other beside him, and I pulled up behind. We hemmed him in and slowed to a stop. I jumped out of the truck and ran to the car, reached in, shut off the engine and waited for the police. Talk about running

"...we all love it when our lives get jolted by something extraordinary, something beyond normal."

60

on pure adrenaline! I'm not going to lie: That chase was exhilarating to the max! It was also a heart-thumping ride for Junanne and the kids.

The funniest thing happened the next evening when I came home from work. As soon as I got out of the truck, my son, Kaben, came running out of the house yelling, "Daddy, Daddy, are we going to chase drunks again tonight?" There was something contagious about the previous night's adventure. We'd become infected by it. Even my bride, who is more mellow than I, thoroughly enjoys retelling this crazy story. Why? Because we all love it when our lives get jolted by something extraordinary, something beyond normal.

BIG HAIRY PROBLEM

Thrill Killer wants to dampen our anticipation of the extra-ordinary. He sometimes talks like a grumpy old man, huffing, "Don't expect too much from life or from God." But he's hawking a lie. He's misrepresenting the God of the Bible. Thrill Killer is content to have us believe in God, so long as we don't expect anything from Him. This impotent deity who is so commonly and impassively worshiped in our dominant Christian culture is lulling us to sleep. What can free us from this lackluster perception of God that makes Him all too puny for far too many?

Thrill Killer loves to invite us, "If you want to really live, you need to make it on your own. God is dull and undependable." This lie needs to be quashed! The fact is that God loves the thrill. He wants to surprise us with twists, turns and adventures. I don't know exactly what He wants to do with you, but I do know that all of us need to live beyond the commonplace of normal. All of us want our lives to count for something significant. We want to make a difference. In order for that to happen, nothing short of God's best plan will do.

Through many years of goal setting, I've learned what it's like to accumulate both victories and failures. I own about 50 books on the subjects of goal setting and getting organized. A common tactic suggested by many writers is to entice people to reach for goals that are a stretch for them, the conventional wisdom being that people won't bother to pursue small goals. A catch phrase that's often used is Big Hairy Audacious Goals. BHAGs are larger than life. But the problem with such goals is that when they're not achieved we can feel defeated. And when we set goals without seeking God and His will, we fail to find the fulfillment and peace we had expected our efforts would bring. The prize at the end of even the biggest goals can leave us empty.

In recent years, I've learned some lessons that can help circumvent the pain that comes from pursuing unfulfilling, humanly devised goals. First, we erroneously think our greatest need is to set Big Hairy Audacious Goals, whereas in reality our supreme need is to align our goals with a Big Holy Audacious God. Before you think I'm disrespecting God, hear me out.

"The prize at the end of even the biggest goals can leave us empty."

The God of the Scriptures is above all other powers. He's able to do amazing things, and His plan is always for our best. The reason we tend to construct our own goals instead of asking for God's input is that we see Him as uninvolved and powerless to give us the quality of life we desire. At great risk to ourselves, we've "created" a puny god who's nothing more than a "consultant" for trivial decisions. We don't dare risk trusting Him with the bigger goals in our lives: our careers, our families, where we live, and more. Instead, we go after what we think will make us happy and later think to ask God to bless our efforts. But it doesn't work because God isn't some kind of cosmic genie! He's so much more.

GOD WITH A CAPITAL "G"

A study of the lives of spiritual giants reveals that we need to begin by accepting God as He is—Big, Holy and Audacious. The plans He has for us are way beyond the normal. The thrill of a life dependent upon God can be realized. And the reward is rich. When we begin our adventure with the God of the universe and ask Him to direct us into His outrageous plans for us, He won't disappoint.

The first step is to practice trusting Him when His plans seem to contradict our own. Consider what Paul believed about our Big Holy Audacious God: "Now to him who is able to do far more abundantly than all that we ask or think, according to the power at work within us, to him be glory in the church and in Christ Jesus throughout all generations, forever and ever. Amen" (Ephesians 3:20–21).

Did you catch that? He's able to outdo all we could ever imagine. I translate Paul's claim like this: "We can ask and we can dream. (And don't stop dreaming.) But the real God will blow our minds by going beyond anything we can ask or dream. As the church learns to follow a totally interested, totally involved God, we'll radiate His greatness." Do you believe this can be true in our time? Does God really want to exceed our individual desires and dreams? You bet He does!

LITTLE-GOD SYNDROME

We admire people who do great things in earthly terms, but when it comes to God we can easily set our sights too low. Could it be that Little-god Syndrome has kept us from the pursuit of truly great things? I know a man who has done more in his lifetime than many of us could even dream of doing. One day I felt bold enough to ask him, "Where is God in your life?"

While pursing his lips and pointing at his shoulder, he announced, "Right here."

I asked for some explanation.

"I call God my little friend," he said. "He sits on my shoulder, and every now and then I ask him things."

> **"I call God my little friend.... He sits on my shoulder, and every now and then I ask him things."**

I half expected to hear God laughing! But this perception of God was no joke to this man. He believes in a tiny god who perches on his shoulder, available at his beck and call. What he describes is more like a glorified Disney character, not the God of the universe.

I respect this man in many ways. He's a model of what hard work can achieve in a capitalistic society. But we've all known people who work hard, achieve much and yet seem to be missing something. The only thing that holds back rich and poor alike from the real thrill is a Big Holy Audacious God.

Before we move on, there are some questions you should ask yourself:

1. Have you a reduced God to a puny, "little-friend" status?

2. Do you see God as detached, as uninterested in you or your circumstances?

3. Do you live as though God were a functionally impotent being, unable to handle the everyday details of your life?

If you answered yes to any of these questions, you've fallen into Thrill Killer's little-god trap, and you're living with Little-god Syndrome. Here are some symptoms of this crippling disease:

VAGUELY ACKNOWLEDGING GOD'S EXISTENCE

Little-god Syndrome says "I believe there is a God" but goes no further. Believing that God exists is easy. It's a belief shared by Thrill Killer. As James, the half brother of Jesus, writes in his letter, "You believe there is one God? So what! Even the demons believe that!" (James 2:19, my translation). Mental understanding that doesn't alter your soul is a little-god trap of deception.

DECIDING THAT GOD IS LIMITED

The little-god mindset says "I won't or can't ask God for that!" This is the some-things-you-just-don't-ask-him-for god. This mentality asks a little god to handle only the little stuff in life. The big stuff is reserved for our own efforts. It's not that we don't want to bother God. Rather, we believe He doesn't want to bother with us. That's another lie from Thrill Killer, and it's absolutely false. To follow this little god slams the door in the face of the true God.

CALLING ON GOD AS THE LAST RESORT

Little-god Syndrome reflects, "I wonder whether God can help me out of this jam." This is the last-ditch-effort god. This is the he's-worth-a-try-when-you-get-in-a-pickle god, or, as every soldier knows him, the foxhole god. We assure him, "God, if you'll get me out of this mess, I promise to do this or that," foolishly believing we can haggle with Him. Honestly, is there anything weaker than a god who can be manipulated? This let's-cut-a-deal approach exposes a tiny-god mentality.

PAYING GOD BACK FOR GOOD THINGS

One of the most destructive symptoms of Little-god Syndrome is declaring "I owe it to God to do this or that. After all, look at what He's done for me." To say "I must serve Him, worship Him and give to Him because of what He's done for me" doesn't demonstrate obedience as much as it displays ignorance or arrogance. What if we *could* pay God back? What do we have to offer Him? What can we bring to the table that He needs, or that He doesn't already own?

> "Whenever we attempt to repay God for His kindness, we present ourselves as His equals. Thinking God wants payback isn't only ignoble—it's naive."

Whenever we attempt to repay God for His kindness, we present ourselves as His equals. Thinking that God wants payback isn't only ignoble—it's naive. If God *needs* us, He's not worth following. Thankfully, even though He doesn't need us, He still loves us and wants to be in a relationship with us. Our worship and service should flow as a result of who He is, not in consequence of what He's done. God deserves our worship and service because He's God— no other reason is needed or valid.

FINDING THE BIG GOD

Today's cultural religion tends to relegate God to life's margins during the week and then to placate Him with a one-hour Sunday visit to church, maybe in conjunction with a small group meeting now and then. I'm convinced that God wants us to live beyond the average or the common. The greatest thrill for us is to encounter the mesmerizing power of Jesus Christ in every moment of every day. This requires finding God. We have to lift up our eyes to catch sight of the God of deliverance, hope and life (Psalm 121). Finding God is a search for the extraordinary. He knows that when we find Him we'll discover what true life is all about. He knows our desire to be vibrantly alive! After all, He crafted us to be remarkable people. And when we invite Him into everyday life, His greatness infuses and transforms everything!

No, I'm not suggesting you have to alter your personality. God loves you just the way He made you. But I am proposing that you invite the Big Holy Audacious God to take over the directorship of your life. You can live a 40-hour workweek life, but don't live a common life. You can live a work-from-home life, but don't live a common life. You don't have to be stuck in a common life with a common god.

When the Big Holy Audacious God enters our lives, we experience a truly thrilling existence. As Big God people, we love when the world hates. When the world hits, we turn to God for guidance on the right response. When the world takes, we give. When the world brags, we boast in God. When the world blames God for suffering, we rejoice in our affliction. That's uncommon, and we could all use a little more of it. But how do we get a clear vision of this Big Holy Audacious God?

CLEAR VISION

I've spent some time in Fresno, California, which is located in the San Joaquin Valley where the Tule fog appears in late fall and winter. And whew! Tule fog redefines your concept of fog. Sometimes it's so thick you can barely see a few feet in front of you. I headed into a patch of it on Highway 99 one morning, and I instantly had to slow to a near stop. The only forward progress I made was when my buddy held open the truck door and watched the white line on the asphalt. He told me which direction to turn the wheel so we could stay in our lane. The crazy thing is that when the Tule fog lifts…Wow! You can see for miles!

"Whether or not we recognize it, we often function as polytheists —people who worship many gods. We "accept" Christ but are continually being lured aside by other little gods."

Catching a vision of God requires allowing Him to guide us out of spiritual Tule fog until the skies open up. Clear vision requires slow and steady rethinking of all our misconceptions about God. He wants us to understand that He's for us, that he loves us and that he has great plans in mind for us. Without this divine vision, people die (see Proverbs 29:18). One reason many don't encounter or experience an uncommon life is that they have a limited vision of what God wants for them. With a clear picture of truth, however, we don't need to hedge our bets about God's ability to care for and complete us.

Whether or not we recognize it, we often function as polytheists—people who worship many gods. We "accept" Christ but are continually being lured aside by other little gods—gods like security, fame, money, sex and anything else that vies for our allegiance. It's hard to admit that we

Big Holy Audacious God

chase after idols, but we all do it. The antidote is focusing on the vision God has for us, a vision that's so grand that all other things become no more than stinking piles of trash in our eyes (see Philippians 3:8).

LOOK AT THAT

The Patriarch Abram, aka Abraham, was one of the first people to catch such a vision. It included a mind-boggling promise, and Abraham's response was a model of authentic faith. "Now the LORD said to Abram, 'Go from your country and your kindred and your father's house to the land that I will show you. And I will make of you a great nation, and I will bless you and make your name great, so that you will be a blessing. I will bless those who bless you, and him who dishonors you I will curse, and in you all the families of the earth shall be blessed" (Genesis 12:1–3).

At first, Abram only "moved his tents." There's something we have to understand about Abram here. He was already elderly and tempted by Thrill Killer to believe that life had passed him by. And his wife was old and barren. Talk about crazy! He had heard the word of God, but the promise seemed so far out there that he was tempted to write it off as one of those weird experiences better left untold. But God wasn't done speaking. A few days later Abram heard from God again, and it knocked him over! To add a little flavor without compromising the story, the encounter might have gone something like this:

"Abram, out of the tent, young man."

"But God, I'm old."

"Out of the tent. Look at the sky. You see that, Abram? Look at the heavens. Count the stars."

"Okay?!"

69

"That's a vision of your future—your legacy," God said. "You'll have more kids than the sky has stars!"

Then in Genesis 15:6, we learn that Abraham "believed the LORD, and [God] counted it to him as righteousness." We all need to get right with God, and as with Abraham, what allows this to happen is abandoning our self and trusting God. This verse is a bedrock of transforming, authentic faith for millions of believers today. Abraham believed—he trusted—and God totally changed his life as a result. This verse is critical because according to Romans 4:11 Abraham is the spiritual father of all believers. God's vision for Abraham, the transformation of his life and his faith in God are the template for genuine faith. The way to know that we've experienced authentic faith is to measure our faith against Abraham's. He modeled clear vision and a thrilling faith worth living.

LEAVING PUNY BEHIND

Abraham's faith was more than some half-hearted mental assent. He heard God's out-of-this-world promises and threw himself to the ground in trusting belief. Abraham's faith was grounded in full-on trust. In Abraham's example we find a compelling truth: *The out-of-this world, high calling of God requires radical faith and a willingness to risk leaving behind the familiar or puny.*

This kind of faith is both energizing and transforming. It begins with utter confidence that God will do what He promises. It says, "God, you describe a transforming power and an unimaginable future for me. It seems crazy sometimes, but I trust You completely with my life." This kind of faith sees the prospect of life with God as more rewarding than the life we're currently living. It calls for a shift in what brings us excitement and fulfillment, a shift in what we worship. My wife called to my attention this quote by Evelyn Underhill: "If God was small enough to be understood, He would not be big enough to be worshipped." And we all worship something. So, are you ready to leave puny behind and be "all-in" with the All-Mighty?

FAITH OF A FATHER

I'm a lot like my dad. I share some of his quirky habits. I love organization, silver-salmon fishing and completing "honey-do" lists for my wife. When I take off my cap, I scratch my head just the way he does. I love the San Francisco Forty-Niners—not just because they're God's favorite team, but because they're my dad's favorite team. In life, we either want to grow up to be like our dads or try hard not to be.

"If God was small enough to be understood, He would not be big enough to be worshipped."

When Paul calls Abraham the "Father of all who believe," he's calling on us to observe Abraham's faith and make it the pattern for our own. God called Abraham to catch a vision for the future that was out of this world—and Abraham believed and acted on that belief. He stayed the course, even when the path got steep and rocky. His faith points the way to the kind of thrilling reality God invites each of us to experience.

BEYOND IMAGINATION

Some things that you passionately desire seem unimaginable. Some of you are praying for the day when a wayward child returns home and is reconciled to the Big Holy Audacious God. Others are imagining your marriage regaining intimacy and moving beyond the "roommate" status into which it's settled. Or maybe you're hoping to find that perfect job or to break free from the addictions that drag you down. Whatever you're dreaming, God is inviting, "Go ahead, imagine and dream. No one else can touch what I've got in mind for you!"

Such out-of-this-world faith isn't wishful thinking or prosperity theology; it's entrusting our lives to the God of the unimaginable. It isn't a calculated way to get something from God or a temporary surrender to see how things might go. Abraham believed that God knew what was best and was willing to abandon all he knew to journey with God into the unknown. Can you say you're willing to do the same? If not, why not?

BEYOND ME

"God, I can't do that" are the sweetest words to God's ears. He loves to hear us admit what He already knows. Until we can stand before Him and declare "I'm trusting you for the stuff I can't do," we won't know what dependent faith feels like. This is why I love the Bible. The common threads woven throughout the Old and New Testaments are amazing. Nearly every person God used to do great things was weak and inconsequential by the world's standards. These impotent, flawed and often clueless individuals definitely needed God to accomplish what He had promised. Together they illustrate that there is no authentic faith, no lasting spiritual transformation, until we come to the end of ourselves and admit "God, I can't do this."

Scripture provides clear direction on how we are to take hold of faith and grab God's uncommon and thrilling vision for us. The steps:

1. Coming to the end of ourselves (Colossians 3:5)
2. Desiring new life in Christ (Matthew 6:33)

3. Acknowledging our sin (Acts 2:38)
4. Finding saving belief (Romans 10:9-10)

These themes can be seen throughout the story of redemption, as unfolded in the Bible. Believing that salvation is something we do *with* God is bogus thinking. The thrill builds when we stop trying to earn salvation by our own power and start relying on God's power. Salvation by faith in God alone is the foundation of the biblical teaching on the issue (see Galatians 2:15-16). This tenet of our faith recognizes that we

> "The battle cry of radical faith is, 'I can't save my life. I can't even make a life. Help me, God!'"

can't provide *anything* to better our situation. The future God has for us is impossible to grasp in our own strength. A faith like Abraham's requires trusting God for the impossible. The battle cry of radical faith is "I can't save my life. I can't even make a life. Help me, God!" This is where thrill finds its strength, and from this vantage point we can watch God do His work. While we can and must certainly partner with Him, we cannot do so in the sense of doing anything effectual for our salvation.

WATCH AND WORK

This whole question of what God does versus what we do has been debated and wrestled with for centuries. James tried to clarify the dance of faith, explaining what God's work is and how we can join Him. He wrote, "What good is it, my brothers, if someone says he has faith but does not have works? Can that faith save him? If a brother or sister is poorly clothed and lacking in daily food, and one of you says to them, 'Go in peace, be warmed and filled,' without giving them the things needed for the body, what good is that? So also faith by itself, if it does not have works, is dead. But someone will say, 'You have faith and I have works.' Show me your faith apart from your works, and I will show you my faith by my works" (James 2:14–18). Let me illustrate the dance of faith and works in this way. As a young man, I had the huge privilege, alongside my dad, of building a new house for our family. I knew very little about construction, but he had a great handle on it. We constructed the whole thing from the ground up. What an amazing summer! Pouring concrete, framing, wiring, plumbing, insulating, dry walling and painting. We did it all. I learned so much, and the reward was over the top because the completed project was a gorgeous, three-story home on a pristine lake in the heart of Alaska. I couldn't possibly have started this project on my own, much less completed it. Every day I'd get up and work alongside my dad. More often than not, I'd watch what He was doing and then join him in that work.

In many respects true faith is like this. God invites us to join Him in a work that will display just how big and incredibly capable He really is. The work He wants to do is in our lives. So we begin by simply watching God. He initiates, and we watch Him to see what He's doing in us or around us; then we join Him in that work. The reason some of us don't know the God of the universe is that we haven't walked with Him, watched Him and then joined Him in the work.

The only way to know the Big Holy Audacious God is through full surrender to Him, through a complete yielding to His vast knowledge and masterful craftsmanship. We watch the Master and then begin to join Him in His work. The result will knock us over. We'll be amazed, just as I was at the end of that summer looking at that fantastic new home. We'll be able to see the hand of God in our lives and will be moved to thank Him for giving us the chance to be a part of something so special and so personal. It's this dance of faith and works that gives us a breathtaking vision of God.

LIFE OF A VISIONARY

Visionaries can be hard to spot. We may think of a visionary as someone with great leadership skills, a loud voice and a commanding confidence. A true visionary, however, is one who is quiet before God long enough to hear and see something revealed that goes beyond personal capacity and comprehension. Here's the greatest news: God has a vision for each of us. You too can be a visionary. And your life as a visionary will exhibit characteristics that validate that you are hearing from God. Visionaries have absolute confidence in God, not in themselves.

"Here's the greatest news: God has a vision for each of us. You too can be a visionary."

Throughout the Gospels Jesus spoke vividly of the kingdom of God. He described life in relationship with Himself in this way: "The kingdom of heaven is like a treasure hidden in a field, which a man found and covered up. Then in his joy he goes and sells all that he has and buys that field" (Matthew 13:44). The vision of the kingdom in this parable was so overwhelming that a man hid the treasure and, in full expectation of the thrill that would eventually be his, liquidated all of his assets to purchase the field with its buried treasure.

If you still doubt the reality of a Big Holy Audacious God and His kingdom, you don't yet have a full vision of life in Him. The thrill and blessing of God are great, and He longs to be generous toward us. Living out God's vision is living out of this world. There is truly no price that can be put on life with God. It's worth more than all we own or could possibly attain in this world. It's a life of true joy.

You've got to start believing. Believe God for extraordinary things, and He'll take it from there. Believe God's ability to prevail over the challenges you face that far exceed your ability to overcome. This isn't some spiritual game or unrealistic optimism. It's belief that surrenders to the God of the universe, rests on the truth of His word and stands back to watch Him work.

This is the God who took Abraham out of his tent and directed, "Look there."

"God, I'm old. And so is my wife."

"She will bear a child."

Unbelievable. Unimaginable.

Yet, totally possible for a Big Holy Audacious God.

Thank God for the faith of Abraham! We can follow his example and start believing God for amazing things in our own lives—things infinitely beyond our most impressive capacities or wildest dreams.

What's holding you back? I invite you, right now, to believe in the God of the universe!

For personal or group study guides and leader support resources, go to www.ThrillOnline.net.

FIVE

TRUE FAITH

I deceive people by allowing them to think they know God.

—Thrill Killer

I've never had anything so mess with my mind as an extended period of sleep deprivation, accompanied with hallucinations, while on the Iditarod Trail. For almost two weeks I'd slept only a few hours a day. The amount of energy expended pushing the sled, along with the long stretches of snowshoeing a trail for my team, had drained me physically. This relentless effort, coupled with grueling, subzero temperatures, had taxed my 18-year old body and mind to the limit.

I'd driven my dogs for hundreds of long miles, and my focus was on their care, not mine. During our stops I spent so much time feeding, watering and bedding them down that I missed the dangerous warning signs my own body was sending. I was pushing myself physically and mentally to a point that was compromising our very survival, without my even realizing it.

One evening, after navigating some hilly terrain, I descended onto the frozen coast of Norton Sound. I was between the villages of Unalakleet and Shaktoolik when the crazy images began. My team was running slowly, and I was exhausted and hungry. Then hope sprung up in my heart at the sight of Shaktoolik on the horizon. As we got a little closer I saw several cabins with inviting smoke curling from their stovepipes. The light from one cabin reflected off the snow and illuminated a man splitting wood. I watched the motion of his swing as he sunk his axe onto the frozen wood with a loud thwack!

There was just one problem.

A little farther on I discovered that the village didn't exist! The cabins weren't there! No one was splitting wood! The images faded, one by one, the closer I got. I stopped my team, set the snow hook and walked toward a cabin, only to have it vanish before my eyes. My mind was playing tricks on me. I was hallucinating. The experience was surreal.

I got back on my sled and somehow managed to keep going. Eventually I found the real village, with real buildings and actual people. But those haunting images were real enough to stick with me to this day.

SPIRITUAL DELUSION

There's a form of spiritual delusion that's similar to my hallucination. We can so desire a spiritual life and the thrill of true faith that we believe we have it even when it's just a figment of our imaginations. Or maybe we want it so badly on behalf of someone else that we convince ourselves that something has happened in them that may not be real at all.

Our world is filled with people who are hallucinating. I'm talking about illusions more dangerous than anything caused by sleep deprivation, alcohol or drugs. I'm talking about the deceptive delusion of *cultural religion*.

Many people mouth the words "I'm a Christian" or "I believe in God." They're comforted by these thoughts and hope that in the end everything will turn out OK. They're holding on, hoping they'll get into heaven. They've taken a hit of the gateway drug "deception." They have just enough religious-sounding stuff to feel good, and the possibility of being spiritually deceived doesn't even cross their minds.

Tragically, these religiously intoxicated people think they're headed for safety, while in reality they haven't been authentically transformed by God. That's the dangerous part of living under the influence. Many are stumbling through life failing to experience God or to live a new and thrilling existence—and, worse yet, they don't even recognize the void. We need the courage to ask an important question: *"Do I and the people I love possess true faith?"*

Jesus talked about the threat of deceptive religious intoxication when He declared that "Not everyone who says to me, 'Lord, Lord,' will enter the kingdom of heaven, but the one who does the will of my Father who is in heaven. On that day many will say to me, 'Lord, Lord, did we not prophesy in your name, and cast out demons in your name, and do many mighty works in your name?' And then will I declare to them, 'I never knew you; depart from me, you workers of lawlessness'" (Matthew 7:21–23).

Consider those words of Jesus, and let their sobering implication sink in. They're not a gentle wakeup call, not a last-minute, pull-it-out-of-the-fire second chance. They're describing the sobering reality of the moment when life is *over*. Jesus, the Messiah, the Christ, the One who paid for sin with His life is talking here, speaking to the ones who did life their way. But their way was way off. And here's the sobering part: Jesus isn't talking to the happy-hour crowd. He isn't dressing down the whores, pimps and gang bangers. He's talking to the culturally religious.

VANISHING HOPES

Jesus' words would've sent His hearers into shock. They had grown up in religious households within a religious system. They preached, taught, served and were active in their synagogues. They were those of whom Paul says that they "[had] the appearance of godliness, but [denied] its power" (2 Timothy 3:5). The response of many on Judgment Day, Jesus says, will be a direct appeal to their past spiritual activity, to their "personal commitment," to the many good things they've done in life. But the soul-shock of lacking true faith is going to be very real when they realize that their good works will do them no good when it comes to salvation.

"Jesus isn't talking to the happy-hour crowd. He isn't dressing down the whores, pimps and gang bangers. He's talking to the culturally religious."

Jesus isn't playing mind games or trying to put us in a state of continuous fear for our souls, but He is giving us a heads-up. He came to make true faith accessible, and His desire is that no one die in a state of spiritual lostness. That's why He didn't mince words or water down the truth. Thrill Killer, on the other hand, tries to make true faith elusive. Thrill Killer deceived people in Jesus' time, and he's still deluding people today.

The good news is that as long as you're alive you can avoid Thrill Killer's ultimate and deadliest trap of eternal separation from God (see Matthew 25:41–46). Nothing, and I mean *nothing*, is more important than taking Jesus at His word. Jesus wants to liberate us from false faith (self-effort) to discover true faith (Jesus' completed work). There are both freedom and thrill in this powerful discovery.

Deception runs just below the surface of our awareness. Thrill Killer loves the clamor of spiritual activity because it can drown out the warning signs of spiritual delusion. The voice of God can be missed when we're too busy to hear it. Thrill Killer loves to let us drink from the cup of religion. The pursuit of religious activities, such as prayer, giving, fasting and serving, when done for their own sake, allows people to believe they're "good with God." If Thrill Killer can keep us focused on those things instead of God, he has succeeded. Then Thrill Killer smiles to himself—because he knows that a spiritually deceived person is a spiritually dead person.

> **"Deception runs just below the surface of our awareness."**

LOVED AND WARNED

There's a graphic and realistic YouTube clip that would scare you to death. It shows a horrific accident that takes the lives of some teenage girls, and it's painfully gripping. The message of the clip is simple: Don't text and drive. The aim isn't just to terrify people but to convince them never again to text while driving, to save them from a grisly death in a car accident.

In the same way, we're both loved and warned by Jesus' words about judgment and eternal separation. God isn't trying to terrify us; He's trying to save us. The picture Jesus paints with His words is born out of His love and passion for people, His longing for them to find true life.

The fact that Jesus shares the future with those who could end up eternally separated from Himself by their spiritual deception reveals two important realities about God. First, duped people matter to God. That's why Jesus came and died for us. Second, deception has dire consequences. Jesus warns us of both the short- and long-term effects of living without true faith.

I'm reminded of a conversation I had with my daughter, Muriel, when she was taking an evening class at a commuter campus. I instructed her to park in a safely lit area, to look around and be aware of anyone who looked suspicious, and to always be ready to defend herself. Did I do this to terrify her? No way! I love her and am aware of the fact that there are people out there who would have no problem hurting my girl if they got the chance. I wanted my daughter to be fully aware of the dangers a woman faces on a big campus at night. Most other fathers would feel the same. The last thing we want is for our daughters to learn "the hard way."

God is the ultimate loving Father. He warns us about spiritual delusion not to frighten us but to manifest His love for us. He isn't playing games or wanting to freak us out. He's passionate in warning us about Thrill Killer's deception because He knows the consequences are deadly.

WHO *REALLY* HAS IT?

Jesus makes it clear that good works and religion don't mean anything if we're missing authentic faith. The Pharisees were self-righteous, but more importantly they were self-deceived—as are many who call themselves "Christian" today. Jesus hammered these obsessively religious people, accusing them of being far from God. On the outside they looked pious, creating for others laws and heavy-handed rules they couldn't begin to keep themselves. They looked "holier-than-thou," but on the inside they were hypocrites. They didn't know God. Worse, they didn't know the love of God, and so they misrepresented Him.

There are still many today who lack true faith. We can think of ourselves as good people, and more especially as good Christians, on the basis of what we do. Some of us are leaders, having grown up in the church and serving faithfully. But here's a hard truth: Passionate decisions, claims of knowing God and even an abundance of good works aren't always evidence of true faith; feelings of righteousness are often misplaced. Spiritual deception is a stealth weapon launched to destroy. Be alert to this subtle but deadly weapon of Thrill Killer.

In the years I've followed Christ, I've found that some of the greatest transformation stories come from people who've been raised in church. The shocking awareness that comes with the revelation that they've never truly known Jesus is real and intense. The realization that they've been living under an illusion of transformation is powerful and sobering. Like someone accustomed to the predictable rides at a kiddy carnival discovering the rush of a high-speed roller coaster, many Christians who discover a transformed life realize that there's no point of comparison between the two experiences. Now they can face life as it really is, with hope and passion, knowing that Christ is working all things for the good of those who love Him.

Junanne and I, along with our entire team, are dedicated to exposing the *Deception of Transformation* through the ministry of Lifelane180, as well as to helping churches reset their thinking in terms of what real transformation is all about. We know firsthand that an apparent Christian experience can sometimes be a deceptive spiritual illusion.

How can this happen? We learn the rules to follow — how to dress, talk, sing and behave, but we don't know the underlying reality. Junanne and I lived this way for years, thinking we were living the Christian life. But we weren't living for Jesus. We were living a form of Christianity without the substance of Christ. We were playing a role in the Christian culture — without true faith. The crazy part is that we didn't even know it!

> "We were living a form of Christianity without the substance of Christ.... The crazy part is that we didn't even know it!"

Maybe people who claim the name of Christ but don't live lives marked by His love and grace have turned you off to Christianity. Thrill Killer loves to turn the spotlight on inauthentic Christians, so as to discredit Christ. But the great news is that God can clear our minds and transform our hearts through an encounter with the real Jesus. He lived a sin-free life and loves people so much that He desires to liberate us from spiritual hallucinations. He wants us safely home, thrilled only in Him. True faith is possible when God lights our way.

FLIP THE SWITCH
Facing reality can be tough. The prospect of you or someone close to you lacking true faith is scary. It's like the dread I experienced as a kid when my folks asked me to go downstairs after dark to get something from the garage. Those few steps into the dark to find the light switch were brutal. But my fear was quickly dispelled the second I could see.

God doesn't want to leave us in the dark. "This is the message we have heard from him and proclaim to you, that God is light, and in him is no darkness at all. If we say we have fellowship with him while we walk in darkness, we lie and do not practice the truth. But if we walk in the light, as he is in the light, we have fellowship with one another, and the blood of Jesus his Son cleanses us from all sin" (1 John 1:5–7).

There's great clarity and hope when God flips the light switch of true faith. What we see won't always be pleasant, but we will be able to discern what's really going on! We can step forward with confidence into the light that will dissolve the dread. I know from experience that when we walk into the light of true faith we'll be able to help others with their fears too. God's Word holds the keys to liberating others from deception. This is what Junanne and I live for—nothing brings us more joy. Now that's a thrill worth pursuing!

THIS IS YOUR LIFE

Jesus was a master communicator. He had a way of attracting large crowds and using parables to get at the heart of each person's story with simplicity and profound truth. One such story, the Parable of the Four Soils, is found in Mark 4:1–9:

> Again he began to teach beside the sea. And a very large crowd gathered about him, so that he got into a boat and sat in it on the sea, and the whole crowd was beside the sea on the land. And he was teaching them many things in parables, and in his teaching he said to them: "Listen! A sower went out to sow. And as he sowed, some seed fell along the path, and the birds came and devoured it. Other seed fell on rocky ground, where it did not have much soil, and immediately it sprang up, since it had no depth of soil. And when the

sun rose, it was scorched, and since it had no root, it withered away. Other seed fell among thorns, and the thorns grew up and choked it, and it yielded no grain. And other seeds fell into good soil and produced grain, growing up and increasing and yielding thirtyfold and sixtyfold and a hundredfold." And he said, "He who has ears to hear, let him hear."

Jesus knew there could still be confusion, so He took the time to fully explain the four soils to His disciples. As you read further, I challenge you with intellectual honesty to identify in these stories the soil that best represents your own spiritual condition. Ask God to shine the light of truth so you can see yourself clearly and even gain insight into the lives of those you love.

THE HARD LIFE

"And these are the ones along the path, where the word is sown: when they hear, Satan immediately comes and takes away the word that is sown in them" (Mark 4:15). Hard-life people are unfazed by the claims of Christ. They're not necessarily hard people as we might imagine them. It's not as though they're all ex-cons with prison tats and sailor mouths. They may be quiet and soft-spoken people or even bubbly socialites. Whatever their personality types, it's their unwillingness to surrender to Jesus that makes them hard.

These people come from every walk of life, but they march to the beat of their own drums. They're often self-made men and women. They may appear to have the world by the tail, or they may endure extended periods of difficulty and tears. What they share in common is that they themselves are the ultimate authorities in their lives.

They have, for whatever reason, shut out God. They may believe that He doesn't exist. They may have been burned by religion or be angry at the deck of cards they've been dealt. They may have been betrayed to the point of wrapping protective layers around their hearts. The irony is that the defensive walls they've built up against God and others are the same walls keeping them from experiencing the thrill they've always desired.

The greatest gift we can give hard-life people is the gift of kindness. They don't need lectures; they need love. I know this because God used His kindness to reach me (see Romans 2:4).

THE SHALLOW LIFE

"And these are the ones sown on rocky ground: the ones who, when they hear the word, immediately receive it with joy. And they have no root in themselves, but endure for a while; then, when tribulation or persecution arises on account of the word, immediately they fall away" (Mark 4:16–17).

Shallow-life people can't survive spiritual storms because they lack a deep connection with God. They're enamored with the promises of what life in Christ *could* be, but they can't sustain their zeal for God. They start strong but sputter out quickly because they haven't tapped in to true faith dependence on God. Some will go through this experience over and over again. They may encounter God at an event, concert, church service or home group and respond by proclaiming, "I'm going for it, God!" Yet Jesus rightly predicted that when something challenges their faith they won't be able to withstand the pressure. When a difficulty comes their way, they'll react with "I'm out."

Shallow-life people have lots of good intentions, but they've never possessed the depth of a transforming relationship with Christ. I know what it's like to have desire while lacking depth. I was raised by great parents, and we attended an awesome little church. I vividly remember the time when a special speaker came to town and told about 20 of us students what Christ wanted for us. His words got us fired up. I was on a spiritual high. I was like, "*Yes!* I want that! I'm going for it!" But within a few days my self-willed attempt to live for Christ fizzled. I hadn't been truly transformed by Christ; I was just emotionally fired up about Him—or more truthfully, about the *idea* of Him.

"I hadn't been truly transformed by Christ; I was just emotionally fired up about Him —or more truthfully, about the *idea* of Him!"

The solution for shallow-life people is to surrender to a deep and close connection with God. Only God can give us the strength to walk with Him and to stand up to the common adversity that comes with true faith. God doesn't want us to be zealous; He wants us to surrender to Himself and allow Him to kindle a sustainable zeal within us (see Titus 2:11–14).

I have a warning for all of us: In our desire for our own selves or for our loved ones to come to true faith, we're vulnerable to being deceived by spiritual experiences. Claims of a "spiritual decision" can lull us into the dangerous delusion of thinking that we (or our loved ones) have true faith when there's been no experience of the power of a transforming relationship with God.

I've seen people come to experience true faith after many years of living in spiritual deception. I've seen their joy when God throws on the light switch of their souls. My hope is that you'll have sound judgment right now. We need the courage to take a hard look at our own and our loved ones' lives, not for the purpose of judging, but to acknowledge that we—or they—may not have true faith. We need to ask God for the wisdom to reach out to our loved ones in kindness—and to address the issues of faith in our own souls—with the truth of the Gospel. It does us no good to lecture or scare someone to "get them right with God" in order that we can feel better about ourselves. The only way to true faith is love. Love those who are languishing in the shallow life, and ask God to give them the real thing.

THE STRANGLED LIFE

"And others are the ones sown among thorns. They are those who hear the word, but the cares of the world and the deceitfulness of riches and the desires for other things enter in and choke the word, and it proves unfruitful" (Mark 4:18–19).

True faith can't get its start in the midst of busy lives twisted up with worry about life, money and pleasure. Growth simply won't happen. God's work can't flourish when the weeds of materialism choke out spiritual interest. Those who place the cares of the world above God have opted for touchable, tangible stuff that may bring, at best, short-term comfort and peace.

Yes, savings and retirement accounts are important, but you can't take them with you when you die. Good health is only temporary. It's the slowest possible way to die, that's all. Managing to look good and successful to others is a waste of time and emotional energy. Keeping your life goals limited to the earthbound kills the possibility of thrill.

The strangled life and the authentic spiritual life can't coexist. Strangled-life people spiritually asphyxiate themselves. The thrill Jesus envisions for us is to live with a constant sense that something eternal and powerful is changing us and those around us. Thrill Killer wants the chains of worry, the crush of wealth and the quest for a meaningful life to exhaust us and stifle anything spiritually productive in us.

"Good health is only temporary. It's the slowest possible way to die, that's all."

The antidote is returning to the one and only source of life—God. Having the seeds of truth planted in the soil of our hearts is the beginning of thrill. If we recognize that we've returned to the strangled life, we need to fall to our knees and ask God, the One Who plants truth, to root out the choking fear or pressure we're experiencing. Once He has prepared the soil of our hearts, we need to ask Him to throw some more seed our way. He's there for us and won't condemn us for the mess in which we're tangled (see Romans 8:1). We can also call a trusted friend and ask them to pray for us and help us if they can.

We have a God who possesses the strength to strip the strangling worries of life clean away. He can neutralize the deception of wealth and bless us beyond imagination in ways so much richer than earthly possessions.

It takes courage to admit that we can see ourselves in these stories of the soil. But it's worth the risk of facing ourselves as we are. Letting God hold a mirror to our lives is the only way to be liberated from deception and to discover thrill.

THE CONTAGIOUS LIFE

"But those that were sown on the good soil are the ones who hear the word and accept it and bear fruit, thirtyfold and sixtyfold and a hundredfold" (Mark 4:20). Contagious-

90

life people have a heart condition that's primed for thrill. They believe that God is infinitely good. They trust God fully and are sponges for truth. They hear the word from God and go His way. This is all done for the purpose of honoring God and enjoying a life that radiates thrill and is truly contagious. Contagious-life people display a calmness and confidence that everything is under control. They live like Jesus, with an obvious love for others and a focus on their well-being.

True faith will ultimately produce people who are thrilled when God uses them. Their impact is real. They possess spiritual strength. Their words convey life. They live for God's glory. He uses them even when the world doesn't see it happening. They experience the thrill and joy Jesus promised in living the contagious life. To lay your head down at night and know that God has directed you is a major release from the clutches of personal effort and worry.

Maybe you're living one of the other lesser lives today but want to live the contagious life, the live consumed with the thrill of God.

You can!

This life is yours if you'll just ask God to lead. Depend on Him. It will be a learning process, and I'm not promising it will be easy, but God is patient with His children. By spending time with God, you'll begin to learn how amazing He is. He'll speak to you as you read verses that show His pleasure in you and as He reveals His plans for your good. As you talk with Him in prayer, whether aloud

"His words paint a picture of a life that is superior to anything we can make for ourselves."

or contemplatively, He'll fill you up with so much of Himself that you'll be enabled to care for others as He does. Jesus wants to touch each of us with words of life. His words paint a picture of a life that's superior to anything we can make for ourselves. He wants His Word to grow in us and to be contagious to those around us.

SWIFT WATER

One summer I went with a large group of friends on a two-day float trip on the Little Susitna River in Alaska. For several of us, the occasion turned into a bit of a race. One thing you quickly learn when racing on a float trip is that the key to speed isn't how hard you work. You can focus on rowing hard, but very little distance is gained by attempting to move a large and loaded raft faster than the surrounding current. The best use of energy is to maneuver yourself into the swiftest part of the river. Once there, stay there.

"The best use of effort isn't in moving forward but in staying off the rocks and away from the trees —in finding the swift current and letting it carry you."

The Little Susitna River is much like the spiritual life. On one side the river is shallow, causing rafts to drag bottom and come to a dead stop. On the other side are overhanging trees that can snag you and bring you to a halt. The best use of effort isn't in moving forward but in staying off the rocks and away from the trees — in finding the swift current and letting it carry you.

That's the way it is with true faith and the contagious life. We can choose to row our way forward with all the effort we can muster, but what a waste! We gain nothing but exhaustion. The essence of a true faith, and the accompanying thrill, is found only in the swift water where God is on the move — in resting in His work and moving forward in His righteousness (see Romans 6). We need to center our lives in that flow. Even this can't be done in our own power but must be accomplished by God's grace. But when we discover that our sole energy expenditure is in moving into the current of His power and allowing Him to do the rest, that changes everything!

For many of us, the spiritual disciplines of prayer, study, meditation and more have been like a weight, draining energy from our lives. I know how this feels. For many years I saw spiritual disciplines as the means of getting farther down the river with God. I thought they would make me stronger and please God.

It never worked.

That's because God doesn't want us to live in our own power or dependent on our own strength to get us moving with Him. Spiritual disciplines get us positioned in order for His power to be unleashed in us. When we pray, study, meditate and engage in other disciplines, we're positioning our lives in God's swift water. His power then carries us along at the pace He sets. His power carries us to spiritual victories. And in His power we anticipate great things around the next bend.

ROCK SOLID

Some of you may be thinking "The Christian life is impossible!" You bet it is! We can't have true faith without dependence on God. Jesus said that people who build their lives on Him and practice what He teaches are like houses built on a rock. Tough times may come crashing in on us, but we stand rock solid if we trust in Christ as our foundation (see Luke 6:47–48).

When I was a young man, I spent time at a friend's commercial fishing site in a little place called Clam Gulch. There are huge tides in that area, tides that can rise 20 feet in less than six hours. Then nothing looks familiar because the seascape changes radically. One day I was staring out across a sweeping vista of mud flats, knowing that in a few short hours they would be swamped by the tide and covered with powerful, swirling seawater.

My buddy looked at me and said, "Hey Karl, you see those huge rocks out there?"

"Yeah."

"You want to name one after yourself? Kind of claim a rock? My buddies and I have already claimed these over here. Go ahead and pick one from over there."

"That one," I said, pointing at a huge rock far out in the flats. "The one way out there. That's Karl Rock."

"Not just yet, Karl," he said. "You've got to be initiated onto Karl Rock. Go on out there, and we'll come get you when the tide comes in."

"I didn't want to die, and I suddenly didn't care about naming the rock—but I was sure glad I had it to stand on!"

Well, I didn't want to miss out on owning my own rock, so I ran on out there and stood up on that big ol' rock. The water was coming in fast. Finally, after what seemed like forever, my friends got into the skiff and came toward me.

"Hey!" I yelled, waving at them frantically. "I'm ready to go!"

They waved back, but didn't come rescue me. They just did loops a quarter of a mile away. Not good. I started getting dizzy watching the water rush in, fast and deep. That tide wasn't anything I could out-swim. The gray silt in the water makes it murky. If you fall in, no one can see what's under the surface to perform a rescue. And the freezing shock numbs your limbs so you can't swim. It can take you down quickly.

Fear exploded through me as I realized that with one slip I'd be a goner. I didn't want to die, and I suddenly didn't care about naming the rock—but I was sure glad I had it to stand on! I closed my eyes as that rocky real estate shrunk around my feet. I crouched down a little bit, recalled to my mind's eye what this rock looked like at low tide. It kept me from panicking until the skiff at last arrived. The rock wouldn't move and I would be all right.

Christ doesn't want us either to fear or to question where we stand with God. We can stand rock solid on His strength (see Romans 5:1–2). The reality is that we can't live out what Jesus has called us to in our own power. It's all about relying on the *righteousness* of Christ. It's not about trying to make our way through self-will. It's about staying in and standing on the *power* of Jesus—the Rock. And it's not the *amount* of faith but the *object* of that faith that gives us the true thrill. Uncertainty will rush around us, but He will save us. That's a rock-solid promise.

So, where are we placing our faith? The contagious life is ours if we surrender our self-will and build our lives in confidence and trust in Christ and Christ alone.

THE JOURNEY BEGINS

Jesus wants us to enjoy life with Him forever. Yes, eternity will be beyond what we can even imagine. God wants to have our hearts today and to take us on an adventure that's an investment in eternity. This journey will be challenging and awesome; it will produce life to the max, along with an infinite amount of joy.

Some of you haven't had true faith. You may be stuck in old patterns that have you discouraged and defeated. Others of you are just plain full of religion—and empty of God. The good news is that there's hope and there's an answer. God wants us to face the life we live, to be honest about our faults and problems, and to turn around and face Him with it all, repenting of the life we've made for ourselves and trusting completely in Jesus.

Repentance is a word that Thrill Killer has twisted. It isn't a word to be used by an angry preacher, as many of us have heard it. Instead, it's a loving and passionate invitation for those who want to live with God. Repentance is an invitation to turn around—a 180 degree turn. It's God's gentle questioning: "Are you done yet? Are you ready to live a contagious life? Are you ready to get into the swift water and take a trip with Me?"

This is the most critical life juncture you'll ever face. Don't leave this world only to have Jesus declare "I never knew you."

And one more thing. Don't compare yourself to others. God's truth is to be the measuring stick of true faith in your life. It could be that many people you thought were poor examples of Christianity don't possess true faith themselves. It could also be that some people are actually derailed disciples who are living the strangled life, unable to show evidence of God's power. God doesn't want you focused on the flaws of others. He wants you looking to Him. Psalm 121:1–3 sums this up beautifully: "I lift up my eyes to the hills—where does my help come from? My help comes from the LORD, the Maker of heaven and earth. He will not let your foot slip—he who watches over you will not slumber."

There's a party going on for God's kids, and He's inviting you. There's a life to live that's far beyond any other, and that's the contagious life. God invites you into the swift current with Him.

TRUE CHANGE

How can you experience this life? Do something humbling and courageous: Confess your spiritual deception to God. This requires simply that you bring to mind the life you've made for yourself and all the ways you've tried to control the outcomes and that you give it all to God, telling Him "I'm done with the life I've made for myself." He loves you—really digs you—and He'll welcome you with a huge hug.

Surrender to God even the shameful mistakes of your past. Jesus has already picked up the tab for your bad choices—all of them, no matter how severe. When Jesus went to the cross, He hung there so that our sins wouldn't be hung on us. As Paul writes in Romans 6:6, "For we know that our old self was crucified with him so that the body of sin might be done away with, that we should no longer be slaves to sin." You've been dragging around your sin long enough now. Whatever sin you can bring to mind, and even the sins you can't remember or have never noticed or acknowledged, have been covered by Christ's blood. He came for you and died for you (see John 3:16).

> "When Jesus went to the cross, He hung there so that our sins wouldn't be hung on us."

Surrender to Jesus' leadership. Ask Him for forgiveness. Find a place to kneel down and pray. Enjoy the power of His forgiveness washing over you. No matter how gross or how trivial your sin may seem, it doesn't have to enslave you any longer. Whether your sin is religious pride or first-degree murder, give it all to Him. He wants to swill a stream of living water through your soul. Let Him know that you're surrendering control to Him. Ask for His joy and power to fill you up. Talk to Him with the words He gives you—they're guaranteed to be words of authentic transformation. Release the shame of the past. Stand tall and walk with Jesus. Discover the thrill you've been seeking.

This is true faith!

For personal or group study guides and leader support resources, go to www.ThrillOnline.net.

SIX

GOD OF BLACK HOLES

**I want every Christ follower to think
they're the biggest loser God ever created.**

—Thrill Killer

I lied to get into Bible College. As I clipped along filling
out the application for Multnomah University, I ran into a
problem. Not a big deal compared to the junk from which
God had already delivered me, but a crisis to be sure. Staring me in the face was this question: "Do you use any
tobacco products?"

Oh, man. Here I was just filling out the application, and
already they were testing me. I figured that if I answered
honestly it would be a deal breaker. So, with a mouth full
of Skoal, I checked the "No" box.

I rationalized my decision. I'd just sworn off binge
drinking and snorting cocaine. I figured a little pinch of
snuff here and there was no big deal. Truth was I chewed
tobacco for breakfast, lunch and dinner, and checking that
"No" box was a blatant lie.

Multnomah accepted me, and I almost forgot about the "No" box incident. But the irony about lies is that even when we seem to get away with them we aren't in the clear. They haunt us. We do everything we can to rationalize, justify and forget them, but they blow in and out of our thoughts, mocking us the whole time.

BIGGEST LOSER

When the day came for me to head north on Interstate 5 for Multnomah University and the cold, wet weather of Portland, Oregon, I felt like such a failure. I was pressed down with crushing thoughts that God was sick of me and my ways. He'd radically cleaned up my life, and yet I couldn't even be trusted to honestly answer a personal question on a college application. Thrill Killer started beating me up by pointing out my recent failings. He reminded me that I'd gone on two weekend binges after I'd told people I was clean by God's grace. I felt as though my whole life was a fraud. The unrelenting guilt led to more shame. I just knew that my failures made me God's biggest loser. Sure, God could help others—but not me.

I was trapped in a downward cycle of sin, sorrow and guilt. I'd mess up, ask for God's help, mess up again, and ask yet again for God's help. I was caught up in a never ending battle that was sucking the life out of me. The thrill of my new life with God was already dying away. I had a mental passion for God, but my shame had me imploding spiritually. I was trapped in a collapsing tunnel of guilt.

As I crossed from sunny, warm California into rainy, chilly Oregon, my guilt rose to a fever pitch. In a moment of disgust I rolled down the window and chucked out my last can of Skoal. I watched it bounce down the highway and off into the long grass on the side of the road. It felt great! In my fresh resolve and zeal I was singing out loud along with my favorite tunes, glad to finally be free of my chewing habit. Surely things were going to be fine now. I may have lied on my application, but this made up for it, right?

For another 20 miles I was on top of the world. I was finished with tobacco. Then it hit me. Overcome with my need for just one more dip, I bolted off at the next exit and headed back to find the can I'd tossed out my car window.

On the side of I-5, I parked my car and ran to the median, searching through the tall weeds for just one more dip of chew. After a few minutes I gave up and trudged back to my car. Emptiness flooded my soul. I was embarrassed and ashamed. I didn't just feel as though I was the biggest loser God had ever created; I knew it. A sudden sense of terrible guilt crushed me as my addiction taunted me. I resigned myself to being a big fat zero in God's eyes.

Have you ever felt this way? No doubt your circumstances are different, but the feeling is similar. That's some big-time pain, isn't it?

Once again, Thrill Killer whispers his lie: "You're the biggest loser God ever created." He's trying to convince us that God doesn't consider us valuable or worth His time. But that's a lie. He loves the messed-up you, unconditionally and completely. God longs to show us just how much He wants us filled to the brim with His life and truth.

CLOSE TO HOME

I've been married to my beautiful bride, Junanne, since 1987. I'd like to tell you it's been all sunny days and sweet-smelling roses, but it hasn't. We both carried a lot of garbage into our marriage. We were told, "Never let the word 'divorce' cross your lips." And we didn't—for two weeks!

> **"We were told, 'Never let the word "divorce" cross your lips.' And we didn't— for two weeks!"**

We had so much to learn and so much to overcome in terms of relational junk. The weight of this, in conjunction with the normal challenges of marriage soured our young love. Sometimes we'd argue till two or three in the morning, really hurting each other. During those fights I said a lot of things that wounded Junanne deeply. Rather than dealing with conflict, we learned to disguise it. We started to live like roommates and not lovers; we started doing our own thing, speaking words of love but lacking true intimacy. We rarely experienced the dream of an ideal life together—what Jesus called us to share. What's amazing now is both how subtly and how far we slid away from each other over time.

I'll never forget the day, a few years into our marriage, when I was walking through our bedroom and Junanne reached up and grabbed my arm. "Bub," she said using her pet name for me, her eyes teary and her lip quivering.

"Yeah, babe," I responded, worried by her tone.

"I've got to tell you something…. I don't love you anymore, and I'm scared to death."

BLACK HOLE

The impact of Junanne's words reached deep inside me, creating a black hole of pain. They weren't spoken in anger; maybe that's what made them hit so hard. The pain from her words tore through my brain and heart all the way to my soul. For the first time in my life, I had no answers.

In a haze, I walked into our bathroom and stared into the mirror. Everything in me wanted to strike back, to unleash a torrent of hurtful barbs and self-justifying accusations. But God spoke to me, saying softly, "Look at yourself, Karl." And I did. I realized I'd spent years subtly stripping my wife of worth with my words, opening unseen wounds that compounded the pain from her past. No physical aggression was needed. My words had done the damage.

Our emotional wounds were fresh, and they infected every aspect of our lives and of our marriage. Thank God, He did bring about healing through our dependence on Him and through long, honest conversations about each other's needs. We dealt with misunderstandings that had grown into hidden bitterness. Discovering the different ways in which each of us had hurt the other was sobering, but it did provide a basis for cultivating healthy communication. Ultimately, our individual passion for God and a commitment to walk together in His truth were the most important ingredients in restoring the health of our marriage.

For some people physical pain doesn't hold a candle to emotional pain. Emotional pain feels like a black hole that sucks the life out of us. Sometimes our black holes are of our own making, while at other times they're created by people and circumstances. I've cried more over emotional, relational and spiritual pain than over any hard-fisted punch I've ever taken. Our pain early in our marriage was a black hole. How would you describe yours?

Everyone has experienced black holes. And when we do, Thrill Killer wants us to believe that God is distant and either unable or unwilling to help us in our pain and trouble. That's another lie from Thrill Killer: He wants us to feel so desperate that we'll believe our black hole is too deep for God to deal with—or that we're unworthy of another rescue. Or even worse, that we have to solve our own problems. Thrill Killer's poison dart of making us doubt that God can or will help us is a lie.

COMPLETELY COUNTERINTUITIVE

I tend to be a solutions guy. I like to get myself and others moving along. My goal is to diagnose a problem quickly and solve it so that I—along with those others who may be involved—don't have to linger in pain or confusion. I try to avoid experiencing the pain of my problems. I find this to be true for most people. No one likes to dive into the black hole of soul-wrenching pain.

Our instinct is to protect ourselves and to survive. Our natural desire is to run away from pain, to avoid the gravitational pull of emotional black holes. I'm talking about the kind of agony that ties the stomach in knots, makes the heart bleed and causes the head to swirl with so many questions we can't even sleep. As a result, we wrestle 24/7 with ourselves, others and even God. In frustration, we emotionally flail while our soul screams into what feels like empty space. In an emotional black hole, the sense of helplessness is profound.

King David, the author of many of the psalms, knew the pain of emotional black holes. He went from being a nobody shepherd to a national hero; from being hunted down by his own hero, King Saul, to replacing him as king of Israel. Then he went from being "a man after God's own heart" to becoming an adulterous murderer who barely survived a coup attempt by his own son. David's poetry explores the deep emotional pain he experienced in life. And his insight into pain is completely counterintuitive. David's solution was to *wait*. Following are a few of his hard-won insights:

> "Wait for the LORD; be strong and let your heart take courage; wait for the LORD!" (Psalm 27:14).

> "Our soul waits for the LORD; he is our help and our shield" (Psalm 33:20).

"Be still before the LORD and wait patiently
for him; fret not yourself over the one who
prospers in his way, over the man who carries
out evil devices!" (Psalm 37:7).

Before we move on, let's consider together these words
of David, setting aside some time to experience this "waiting." Think about something going on right now, something you've tried to move beyond but that keeps draw-
ing you downward into your black hole. Look for the part
of your story that's broken, incomplete or unsatisfied. Is
it a dismal failure of a marriage, a depressed child or personal anxiety? Is it a betrayal by a long-time friend or the
loss of a treasured dream? We all have black holes. Maybe
yours is so overwhelming you can't even put a name to it.
You have no answers, nowhere to go and no one to whom
to turn. Maybe it feels as though God is light years away.
Now I want you to understand one thing: *God isn't light
years away; He's closer than you can imagine.* And He desires
to be the solution to your black hole.

WAITING FOR WHISPERS

I've learned experientially that waiting on God involves
admitting that I'm in need of a savior and allowing myself
to feel the distress of my soul. The prophet Isaiah spoke
candidly of the God who meets us in our black holes.
He wrote some incredible words of encouragement for
the times when we feel the pain of living in a black hole:
"Blessed are all those who wait for Him!" (Isaiah 30:18).
I would translate this as "God visits black holes, and He
brings joy.... Just wait for Him." For those of us in the dark-
est black holes, the waiting is the hardest part. Without the
certainty of relief, we tend to scramble for any resolution.

But scrambling people never see God; they just get more and more hopelessly entangled in their mess.

Having traveled thousands of miles on a dog sled, I've been lost several times in pitch-black, starless nights. I've spent hours searching in the dark for the right trail and have exhausted more than one team of dogs groping for the way forward—or the one that leads back home. After several frustrating experiences, I learned that it's better to wait a few hours for sunrise than to risk getting farther off course.

"After several frustrating experiences, I learned that it's better to wait a few hours for sunrise than to risk getting farther off course."

It's the same way for us in life. God says, "All your scrambling in the bewildering darkness will only exhaust you and leave you in a worse place. Wait!" The reality is that God is in our black holes with us, whether or not we realize it. One of the most powerful stories of God's presence relates how He spoke to Elijah in a dark cave when the prophet was running scared from the wicked queen Jezebel: "And [God] said, 'Go out and stand on the mount before the LORD.' And behold, the LORD passed by, and a great and strong wind tore the mountains and broke in pieces the rocks before the LORD, but the LORD was not in the wind. And after the wind an earthquake, but the LORD was not in the earthquake. And after the earthquake a fire, but the LORD was not in the fire. And after the fire the sound of a low whisper" (1 Kings 19:11–12).

God was in the whisper. Elijah's experience of being met by God in his fear and failure is profound. God often speaks into our lives in a whisper. To hear that voice we must be still, waiting before God. And when we hear Him, everything changes.

PAIN RELIEF

The thing about tears is that they never dry up until we deal with our pain. That's what God promises for those who wait on Him and call for His help: "For a people shall dwell in Zion, in Jerusalem; you shall weep no more. He will surely be gracious to you at the sound of your cry. As soon as he hears it, he answers you" (Isaiah 30:19). What a great God we have. We know that while we may experience deep pain in our hearts, a time is coming when that pain will be no more. Until then, we must wait and take refuge in our God.

God won't reject a desperate and humble heart. His ear is honed in to our cries. "The high and lofty one who lives in eternity, the Holy One, says this: 'I live in the high and holy place with those whose spirits are contrite and humble. I restore the crushed spirit of the humble and revive the courage of those with repentant hearts'" (Isaiah 57:15, NLT). No matter what pain we face today, no matter what the depth of our personal black hole, God is here to speak to our hearts and minds.

> "God inhabits black holes even when we can't see or feel Him. When there's nothing else, He is our everything!"

God inhabits black holes even when we can't see or feel Him. When there's nothing else, He is our everything!

VOICE COMMANDS

I must have murmered to myself a hundred times, "If only God would just tell me what to do!" Aren't you glad that God has deeper, more personal communication channels than Twitter or Facebook? The Old and New Testaments reveal deep truths about how we are to live our lives. They're an amazing revelation of God's voice. Victory is discovered when we learn to distinguish His voice from that of Thrill Killer.

Jesus warned His followers to look out for wolves in sheep's clothing. He directed us to focus on Him and His voice: "My sheep hear my voice, and I know them, and they follow me" (John 10:27). By listening to Jesus' voice through the Scriptures, as well as when it comes to us from God-fearing, God-loving folks speaking into our lives, we can begin to climb out of our black holes into the light-filled, thrilling life in Jesus. We must follow God's voice out of our black holes; there's no other way out.

This reminds me of the times when I talked to my lead dogs when no trail existed and yet I knew where to go. I guided my little leaders with voice commands as they trotted along, calling "Gee" (right), "Haw" (left) and "On ahead" (keep going straight). My encouraging voice would direct them to the right path and away from the dangers of being lost in the wilderness.

God doesn't yell. He doesn't compete with the common noises of our day. But when we turn down the volume of the world, become still and silently wait on God, we can hear Him speak. At what points in your life do you feel as though you're missing the path? Are you having trouble connecting with your child? Has your marriage been de-railed? Are you secretly addicted to something that's destroying you? Maybe you've reached a "Y" in the road in terms of a business, a relationship or something else about which you need to hear from God. Listen closely for His voice of truth. He enjoys directing us into the path of thrill, and He won't play hard-to-get.

How awesome that God finds us in our black holes and with a gentle voice leads us out into His light!

NEW PASSION

When God meets us in the darkness of a black hole, something amazing happens. We see what we couldn't see before, enjoying a fresh perspective and a heightened awareness. We may not be free from all our pain, but God shines a light on our world and lets us know that He sees and cares about how messed up it is (see 1 John 1:5).

Sometimes we can clearly see the steps that led us into our black hole: pride, blame, lust, apathy, lack of forgiveness and other sins. We can't take our sin with us into the light of God, and thankfully His love helps us leave those things behind. He illuminates our lives and reveals the stuff that needs to be repaired, replaced or discarded (1 John 1:7).

We can also see the ways in which God uses the sin of others for our good. We can understand the compassion of Joseph, a young man who was sold into slavery by his own brothers. He saw the bigger picture and didn't let bitterness take hold of him. It was the whisper of God that enabled Joseph to say years later to those very same brothers, "As for you, you meant evil against me, but God meant it for good, to bring about that many people should be kept alive, as they are today" (Genesis 50:20). When we hear God's voice, we have the opportunity to respond with absolute trust and passionate faith.

SMASHING IDOLS

When God pulls us out of black holes, He simultaneously reveals our idols to us. Idols are anything we substitute for the life that is to be found in God alone. We can make idols out of anything. As pastor Tim Keller expresses it, "An idol is taking a good thing and making it an ultimate thing." Idols are generally born out of our passions—passions not guided by God. We take

"An idol is taking a good thing and making it an ultimate thing."

things that are often good in themselves, like shopping, sex, food, TV, social networking or sports, and make them "The Thing" that makes us feel alive. As a consequence, our lives, families and budgets are turned upside-down.

Living a life in God is a narrow path, and the only way to get on that path is by doing a 180-degree turn. We're born going the opposite direction from God, but He calls us to turn around and draw near to Him. That's not to say that we won't experience pain or find things we still need to work on. The point isn't instant perfection but the journey itself. Jesus uses our journey to make us continually more like Himself.

Along the way, we may stray off course and need to make adjustments. I have discovered that even my passion for seeing people's lives changed can become an idol. Wanting to see people transformed is a good thing, and the more power of God I see in others lives, the more I want to turn people on to Jesus Christ. But I need to guard against taking the good thing of ministry and making it "The Thing." I've learned that when I hang on to ministry too tightly I can hurt people.

As a leader, I've been guilty of micromanaging my staff in my passion to reach lost people. Even though I didn't intend to offend or injure anyone, I did. After being confronted I was brokenhearted at the pain I'd caused. And after seeking forgiveness, I've discovered three things: God will use messy and painful circumstances to tear down idols in our lives. We must be willing to do anything God asks to seek peace. God gets glory from situations much differently than we can ever imagine.

I may always battle to keep ministry in perspective and to resist idolatry. In case you think that sounds noble—it isn't. We all battle against allowing things that are perfectly good in themselves to become idols. We bust our tails and may come to idolize work. We relax and are tempted to idolize time off. We can idolize substance, beauty, fame, drink and, well—you name it and somebody, somewhere, has probably made an idol of it. We'll always battle idols, but when God hears our cry for help He steers us away from sin and leads us to finding our satisfaction and thrill in Himself.

NEW PERSPECTIVE

A "healthy" perspective on sickness would say that its up side is getting better. Even feeling 80 percent better seems like a "new you" after a case of the flu. Likewise, the greatest thing about a black hole experience is coming out of it. When God rescues us from our sin and its effects, we experience the sweet spot of walking with Him. His whisper leads us out of our black holes and into the thrill of a wholesome relationship with Him and others.

I can promise you that fulfillment is on the way, but for some of us the days of waiting will be long. As with Joseph, the realization of God's provision is found for many of us through a process of suffering rather than in instant deliverance. We can't predict the means by which God will rescue us, but we are promised that He will. Why? Because the heart of God is to lovingly care for His creation. As Jesus puts it,

"Look at the birds of the air: they neither sow nor reap nor gather into barns, and yet your heavenly Father feeds them. Are you not of more value than they?" (Matthew 6:26).

We may not be clear of all the pain, and we may not be at full strength and completely confident in Christ, but, oh boy, how our perspective changes when we experience the radical, saving power of Jesus! An old saying has it that "God is in the business of turning wounds into sacred scars."

"God is in the business of turning wounds into sacred scars."

I really like this saying. Wounds represent pain that's still in process; scars represent healed injuries that remind us of lessons learned. Scars are the evidence of God's healing.

STILL WAITING

Another tried and true saying reflects that "God's never late, but He's rarely on our time." God's timing is always perfect, but that doesn't mean He'll move when we think He should. That's because our all-about-us perspective is narrow and limited. As Peter writes, "But do not overlook this one fact, beloved, that with the Lord one day is as a thousand years, and a thousand years as one day" (2 Peter 3:8).

We often act on feelings rather than on facts. We feel as though God must have missed the details in our lives that need addressing. So we run ahead with our own fix-it ideas. But it pays to pause and recall that God—not any of us—has the best answer for our lives. He alone has a complete perspective. We see life from a miniscule point of view, but if we have the strength to wait and trust, He *will* heal us.

When God doesn't respond according to our timetable, we're the ones who are off, not God. If we practice waiting instead of reacting during a crisis, we'll save ourselves and others a lot of heartache. I've seen this happen hundreds of times. The longer I live, the more confident I am that God's direction and timing are impeccable.

In times of pain and chaos, staying put and resisting the urge to jump the gun can seem like the craziest thing to do. I know. As our adrenalin pumps in a crisis, every urge within us insists, "I've got to do something!" I invite you, in response, to consider this truth: Waiting on God *is* doing something. A simple prayer, advising God that we're surrendering to His control, is a great way to wait. "God, I give up.... Meet me in this place." Prayer and waiting go hand in hand.

Another thing we can do as we wait is to confide in a trusted friend about how we're feeling. Be honest, speaking from the heart. Sharing our black hole experiences and just knowing that someone else is praying for us can provide relief. When I find myself in a black hole, it helps most to walk and talk with God. Getting air into my lungs can clear my mind and make it easier for me to hear God's voice.

Remember this: *God isn't playing games with us, and He's never late.* That's the promise given to us in Isaiah 30:18: "Therefore the LORD waits to be gracious to you, and therefore he exalts himself to show mercy to you. For the LORD is a God of justice; blessed are all those who wait for him." I love it that He cares about justice even more than we do. My best advice, then: Wait on His voice and watch His plan unfold.

THE GAP

There's a place none of us would choose to live: I call it The Gap. It's the place of waiting on God. Waiting can be painful and even cause us to ask questions about God's resolve or ability to deliver on His promises. But it's there within The Gap that we learn dependence and grow in maturity. No spiritually great man or woman has ever avoided The Gap.

Every successful marriage has spent time there. And anyone who wants to impact the world must journey through it.

The Gap is the place where we wait…and wait…and wait. And just when we think we've waited long enough, God has a way of stretching out The Gap. Ironic as it may seem, He does this because He loves us so much and knows that utter dependence upon Himself is the only way we can survive and thrive in this world. Whatever you do, never run from The Gap. Stay and wait; God always delivers! "And thus Abraham, having patiently waited, obtained the promise" (Hebrews 6:15).

WAIT AND SEE

I never did recover that can of Skoal I tossed out the car window on I-5, but God found me there in my black hole of addiction and shame. I cried out to Him, and, not surprisingly, He showed up, picked me up and whispered in my ear that He would help. I wept for miles as I headed toward campus. He saved me from that sin, and He's done the same with regard to many more since. Here's the good news: God meets us in black holes every day. This is, after all, a fallen and broken world, with new challenges coming our way all the time. But a new heaven and new Earth are in our future— and black holes don't exist there! (Revelation 21:1-2).

Our problems and pain may be bigger than we are, but they're never too big for God. He specializes in delivering people from "impossible" situations. God can remove any black holes that have engulfed our lives. He can renew the thrill we once had in Him. Just wait and see.

For personal or group study guides and leader support resources, go to www.ThrillOnline.net.

SEVEN

BFF

**I want people to feel alone and
without a friend in the world.**

—Thrill Killer

The toughest thing I did as a young pastor was to tell a woman that her daughter had just been found dead. As I stood at the door that evening and gave her the horrible news, she collapsed onto her entry floor and sobbed uncontrollably. I knelt down and held her in my arms—it was the only thing I could do. The news of her daughter's death overwhelmed her. I could barely bring myself to tell this grieving mom that her girl had committed suicide, because I knew the grief and anguish this would cause.

She had many questions, and I had mine too. They bombarded my mind. What could have caused this young woman to become so desperate? Was there more I could have done to prevent this from happening? What was going through her mind in the last moments of her life?

Suicide is the ultimate bait and switch. Some people believe that ending it all is worth the promise of no more pain. Others consider it a way to get back at or to punish someone else. This young lady, and anyone else who takes his or her own life, had been sold a seductive pack of lies from Thrill Killer. He isolates hurting people and then catapults them with feelings of loneliness and hopelessness. Without a safe outlet to help unload the nonstop negative feelings and fears that poison the mind, the pain can escalate beyond endurance.

It's a common tactic of Thrill Killer to sell us the lie that no one wants to hear about our pain. He wants us to believe that even our close friends would be scared off or disgusted by the truth of our thoughts. He wants us to feel alienated because we think nobody understands or can really help us. When our sense of self-worth is shredded, evil can distort our view of the short-term future, making the "escape" of suicide or some other destructive solution sound appealing.

The sad thing is that for every person who takes his or her own life, there are millions more who, though technically living, aren't fully alive. As William Wallace put it in the movie *Braveheart*, "Everybody dies; not everyone really lives." How tragic that many people lack a passion for living. This deficit is usually compounded when they feel as though no one understands or cares.

A deep desire of Thrill Killer is to get us thinking that God is too busy or too holy to help us, that we're on our own. If this is our view of God, how can we possibly expect Him to see us through the deepest challenges we face?

TURNING POINT

Thrill Killer wants us never to think about God, let alone turn to Him. If you do think of God, Thrill Killer wants you to blame Him for everything that seems wrong in your life. Much to the contrary, we need to expose and untangle Thrill Killer's knot of lies. We can't do this in our own wisdom or understanding, but it's a great threat to Thrill Killer when we begin to understand the greatness of God and to recognize how personal and trustworthy He is. God wants us to lean on Him and resist trusting in our own ability to understand the intricacies and twists of life, as He opens up a straight path in front of us (see Proverbs 3:5-6).

I've learned a tough lesson: A renewal of true thrill is sometimes best cultivated through our bleakest times. When vitality is sucked out of us and we can't seem to draw anything out of life, we're actually at a turning point. And that's a good place to be. It seems odd, but in the economy of God's kingdom there are numerous reversals of our natural ways of thinking. The last will be first, the foolish will confound the wise, and the broken will be the real winners (see Matthew 5:3). Strength and deliverance from any situation are always and only found in dependence on God.

"When vitality is sucked out of us and we can't seem to draw anything out of life, we're actually at a turning point."

ON TARGET

Some dogs leave a mark on your life. In my short couple of years of preparation to compete in the Iditarod Trail Race, I gathered a great team of dogs, each of which had his or her unique personality. Over the course of thousands of miles together, I learned that it's one thing to have a dog that *obeys* you, but it's something else entirely to have a dog that *understands* you.

I got my first dog, Target, from the pound. She was a shy Alaskan Husky about to be put down, and when I took her home it was as though she knew I'd saved her from death. I treated her like family and took her everywhere. The first time I tried to put her in harness she didn't understand what I wanted from her. She wouldn't run or pull. The problem was that all she knew was to stay close and hang with me. When I moved, she'd move; she never wanted me out of her sight.

One day I tricked Target into discovering that she was born to run. I hooked her into a team of dogs and ran down the trail a good distance ahead. Then my mentor, who was helping me train the dogs, cut them loose. Target practically ran over the other dogs in her frenzy to reach me. As the team shot past, I stepped out of a stand of trees where I'd hidden and hopped onto the runners. By the time Target saw me on the sled behind her, it was too late. She was hooked on the joy of pulling a sled. She had learned that she was born to run.

Target didn't have the drive or the smarts to lead a team of dogs. But one cold winter day, during my first long-distance race, she saved my bacon. My team of 12 dogs ran hard for the first 30 miles. The trail was frozen, hard and fast, and I couldn't slow the team as much as I would have liked. As a consequence, my dogs became exhausted far too early. Much farther on, when we came to the foot of a steep hill, my lead dogs stared up that daunting slope, threw in the towel, so to speak, and sat down. The rest of the team followed suit, plopping to the ground.

I spent a couple of hours switching out dogs up front, but not one showed a willingness to run lead. Because I was too young to enter the race, I'd petitioned for a waiver and had been granted one. This added to the pressure I felt to complete the race. I didn't want those who had told me I was too young to be proven right! As I rotated through the dogs, it grew darker and colder by the minute. Despair began to set in and altered my short-term view of the race. This defeat would certainly derail my dream of running the Iditarod.

I'd tried every dog but one—Target. At my lowest emotional point she was my only hope. I looked at her and said, "Target, girl, we're in trouble. Could you help us out?" You might think I'm crazy, but she looked at me as though she understood. I took her from the back of the team and marched her to the front, praying this would work. I gave the command, and she leaned into the harness and pulled the weary dog team to its feet. For 30 more miles she led the team with all her might, looking back only once as though to say, "I knew we were in a jam; you can count on me to get us out of it!"

I was clapping, singing and shouting praises at her; and she knew it. We arrived safely at the checkpoint well after the other teams—but thankfully we did arrive. Target never ran lead again. She'd accomplished her most heroic task. She understood my need that night, and I loved her for her one-time heroic effort. The infinite friendship of God can't be compared to that of a dog. But Target's devotion has remained for me a picture of God's commitment to us when we're in a tough spot.

In the text lingo of the Twitter Age, God is our BFF (Best Friend Forever). He's there to pull us through even when we, and everyone around us, are ready to quit. God wants us to know that He comes through for us even though we don't always

> "In the text lingo of the Twitter Age, God is our BFF (Best Friend Forever)."

recognize or acknowledge it. He has perfect timing and an ideal way of dealing with every situation. He not only invites us to a thrilling life; He rescues us when everything seems to be grinding to a halt.

WHEN GOD SHOWS UP

God's desire is to be present and active in our lives. When we're stuck, stalled and primed for another failure, God is ready to re-script what's about to happen—if we're bold enough to ask Him to be our leader. When our plans don't work out, we can find ourselves in the cold, dark night, calling desperately for clear direction. That's when God confirms for us His love and power. He sees through the deepest darkness, and despite the toughest conditions He pulls us to our feet and gets us moving again.

When life is empty and we're at our worst, God often shows His best, and He does so through His Son, Jesus Christ. Jesus wasn't sent to help us but to save us. The incredible friendship of Christ is experienced most emphatically when we're down—and I mean way down. He heals wounds, untangles relationships and refreshes our self-perception. His mercy to us allows us to be merciful to others. The fresh, clear thinking he instills within our minds triggers hope and a desire to press on.

BELOW THE SURFACE

The writer of Hebrews describes Jesus in an amazing way: "For we do not have a high priest who is unable to sympathize with our weaknesses, but one who in every respect has been tempted as we are, yet without sin" (4:15). How great a best friend is that! No matter what we're going through, Jesus can empathize with our weakness. Because He was human, He can identify with us, understanding exactly what we're going through. He knows what it's like to be lonely, abused and betrayed. He understands the struggles we face and how they make us feel.

Savor this realization for just a moment. It's like a ray of sunshine or a breath of fresh air in a musty room! This realization opens us up to new truths about how God relates to us. It presents fresh possibilities for the future. However, something more needs to happen. We need to go below the surface and see how and why God empathizes with us.

I fished commercially in Bristol Bay, Alaska, for 8 seasons. The adrenaline of catching nearly a hundred ton of red salmon each season was over-the-top. Every day had its own surprises. The weather could be nasty. At the peak of the season, we could work for days on end with precious little sleep. We fished out of 32-foot boats. Our nets were three hundred yards long and about twelve feet deep, with "corks" along the surface. The water was cold and dark. The only way we could tell whether we had any fish was when a cork would bob on the surface.

What a thrill when the whole length of net had bobbing corks! This was the tell-tale sign that we had hundreds of valuable fish in our net. Once the activity on the surface slowed, we'd start hauling in the gear. Now the fun began. As we pulled the net over the stern, we could see our amazing catch. Those shiny fish would just come flipping out of the ocean into our little boat. At times they would be so thick that we'd find ourselves stuck, knee high, in thousands of pounds of fresh catch. We'd high-five each other and yell at the top of our lungs. It was a total rush!

Catching truth should be similar to fishing in Bristol Bay. The truths that Jesus relates to us are like bobbing corks on the surface of the water. There is more, much more below! The Scriptures are loaded with vivid details about how Jesus lived and how His life relates to ours. We need to pull in these truths and catch the deep lessons waiting below the surface. Discovering truth is thrilling!

BEST FRIEND

When you feel as though you don't have a friend in the world, don't let Thrill Killer's lies deceive you. The truth is that you have a Best Friend, and His name is Jesus. He knows what it's like to experience sibling rivalry, grueling physical work, bullying by powerful people in authority, and even betrayal. Rejection by family and close friends brought deep heartbreak to Him (see Matthew 26:40-42).

Listen! When we're most needy, Jesus is most relevant (check out Hebrews 4:14-16). He knows what life is like on Earth. He lived here, ate here, worked here, ran into jerks here and faced everything we do (well, with the possible exceptions of bad drivers and slow downloads). As David Needham writes in his book *Close to His Majesty: An Invitation to Walk with God*, "What you need is more than forgiveness. You need someone who understands you and your situation well enough to point the way out. Wouldn't it be tragic if at the very time you needed God the most you couldn't reach Him? But He is there, ready to listen. He's someone who knows you far better than you know yourself."

"He lived here, ate here, worked here, ran into jerks here and faced everything we do."

There are several truths about Jesus' human experience that bring us fresh light and hope. Let's take a closer look at some of them to see where we can identify.

BEEN TIRED?

Jesus got tired. In His short life Jesus walked thousands of miles to minister to the hurting. On one particular journey to Galilee through Samaria, Jesus had been walking in the hot sun for hours when He came to a well. As John tells us, "Jacob's well was there; so Jesus, wearied as he was from his journey, was sitting beside this well. It was about the sixth hour" (John 4:6).

For me, this means that I have a God who understands how I feel when I'm exhausted. And I mean spent. We all have things that beat us down and wear us out. For myself, I don't know anything more exhausting than raising kids—at least if you hope to do it halfway right. Junanne and I have two grown kids. We love them, but that doesn't mean that parenting was easy—or, for that matter, that it's ever really over. Reasoning, arguing, broken boundaries, surprises from bad grades, banged-up cars—all of these trials take it out of you as a parent, even when your kids are as awesome as ours.

You know what Jesus says to all of us parents? After a full day of wrestling with two-year-olds or teenagers, we can count on Him knowing how tired we are. And He offers rest and wisdom (see James 1:5). He assures us that instead of carrying the burdens and responsibilities alone, we can place them on Him and rest: "So then, there remains a Sabbath rest for the people of God, for whoever has entered God's rest has also rested from his works as God did from his" (Hebrews 4:9-10).

If you're overwhelmed and overtired to the point that rest and sleep are elusive, know that Jesus has been there and models an example of a balanced life. He certainly worked hard, but He also rested. The Gospels are full of stories that depict Him eating, relaxing and enjoying life with His friends and disciples. There are also stories of Him going off to be alone and to rest in God through prayer. We benefit from following His pattern.

> "There are times when napping might be the most effective way to honor God.... In doing so, we acknowledge that He can get by without our help for a while."

It used to be my goal to get by on as little sleep as was reasonably possible. As I became a more mature follower of Jesus, I realized that this was wrong-headed. Jesus modeled that tired people need to rest their bodies and spirits. (Before reading any further, feel free to take a nap.) There are times when napping might be the most effective way to honor God—really! After a full day of doing the "good works" God has designed for us to do (see Ephesians 2:10), he calls out to us, inviting us to just *rest*. In doing so, we acknowledge that He can get by without our help for a while.

BEEN MISUNDERSTOOD?

Have you ever been misunderstood? It can be humiliating, frustrating and downright maddening. Everywhere Jesus went He was misunderstood—even by His disciples, those who should have known Him the best! Listen to the summary in John 12:16: "His disciples did not understand these things at first, but when Jesus was glorified, then they remembered that these things had been written about him and had been done to him." In other words, Jesus walked through this world doing things and living fully in tune with God's plan, even though people didn't understand His actions.

Maybe you've thought, "I wish I could somehow convince others that what I'm doing is right. I'm really not crazy." Junanne and I know a Christ-following young woman who's married to a man who thinks she's a fool because of her beliefs. She is verbally attacked because of her faith in Jesus. Her husband tells her that she's weak; he doesn't understand her need for God. Because of this divide, she can't tell him about her deep friendship with God. How painful for this young wife to daily pray, weep and hope that the love of her life, the father of her children, will stop ridiculing her faith and come to know God the way she does.

> "I wish I could somehow convince others that what I'm doing is right. I'm really not crazy."

We've all been misunderstood. But I want you to know at the deep-down, gut level that you've got a Best Friend Forever in Jesus. He gets you. He loves you. He's there to comfort you. He understands how the fallout of a broken culture permeates the world. He's the God who sees, and He's at every moment of every day intervening and limiting the pain of being misunderstood.

BEEN BETRAYED?

The pain of betrayal is especially brutal when it's caused by a friend. And the reason the pain is so deep is that only a friend has the power to betray us. When someone who knows us at the soul level chooses to take us down, the result is devastating.

Jesus ran around with 12 guys into whom He poured His very life. They'd seen Him work miracles of all kinds. He'd opened their eyes to the truths hidden in parables that others never understood. He'd washed their feet and served and loved them for three years. They'd eaten together, traveled together, suffered together, prayed together and most certainly laughed together. Of all the people in the world, these 12 men were the closest to Him.

Yet one of these friends betrayed Jesus, and the rest denied Him. Judas even took a bribe from the authorities, who hated Jesus. As though betraying Jesus weren't enough, Judas made it personal and even more cruel by using the gesture of a kiss to single out Jesus so the soldiers could take Him down: "While he was still speaking, there came a crowd, and the man called Judas, one of the twelve, was leading them. He drew near to Jesus to kiss him, but Jesus said to him, 'Judas, would you betray the Son of Man with a kiss?'" (Luke 22:47–48). Can you hear the pain of betrayal in Jesus' words? Some of you know how it feels to have a friend stab you in the gut as he kisses your cheek. Jesus knows your pain.

> "Some of you know how it feels to have a friend stab you in the gut as he kisses your cheek. Jesus knows your pain."

If you've read or viewed on screen *The Count of Monte Cristo*, you know that the story touches a raw nerve in all of us. It's the depiction of a devastating betrayal at the hands of a friend. In the count's case, the betrayal was at two levels: One with the childhood friend who frames him for treason in order to steal both his wealth and his sweetheart, the other with a politician who uses his authority to pervert justice in order to preserve his own career.

When a friend betrays us, it's painful, but when those in authority betray us it can be devastating. When authorities allow lawlessness to go unchecked, it leaves us with no one to turn to but God. It's not a problem for Him to take on the pain we can't bear. We can call on Christ to step into our lives and heal the wounds inflicted by backstabbers. Justice is in His hands. He's able not only to heal the wounds of betrayal but to use the scars to comfort and help heal others.

BEEN TEMPTED?

Temptation has different tugs and triggers for each of us, but everyone experiences it — even Jesus did: "Then Jesus was led by the Spirit into the desert to be tempted by the devil" (Matthew 4:1). Yet despite being tempted, he was without sin (see Hebrews 4:15).

Satan, not God, sets up the temptation trap (James 1:13). He wants us to feel guilty for feeling tempted. But being tempted isn't a sin! Jesus was tempted in every way and yet was without sin. Knowing that He was tempted in *every way* tells me that there was a continuous barrage of temptation going on in His life. He was hammered by spiritual, material and even sexual temptations. Temptation isn't sin — giving in is. When we understand that Jesus was tempted but without sin, we can have confidence that He who overcame every temptation not only isn't surprised by the crazy thoughts coursing through our minds but is ready to strengthen us in our fight.

Thrill Killer wants to disqualify us from all the good plans God has for us by defeating us through false guilt. The chief weapon in his arsenal is deceiving us into confusing temptation with sin. But we don't have to feel defeated just because we're tempted. When we do give in to temptation, we experience true guilt. But because of Jesus' work on the cross, we have a good and gracious Savior Who forgives us as we confess and come clean from the junk in our hearts (see 1 John 2:1).

Men, I need to talk with you personally for a moment. The solo effort to avoid temptation can so exhaust us that we actually make ourselves more susceptible to sin. Let me illustrate this with sexual temptation.

Here's how it went for me. Thoughts and fears about the possibility of sinning would drive me crazy. Thrill Killer caused me to condemn myself falsely over and over again. I couldn't enjoy a life of victory when my mind was eaten up with the guilt of temptation. Thankfully, I finally learned that God never condemns me for temptations to sin. Have I ever given in to temptation? Yes. Admitting my sin makes me grateful for my friend, Jesus, Who forgives unconditionally. But temptation needs to be seen for what it is. If you're tempted, acknowledge where it comes from, ask for protection for your thoughts, confess the battle to a trusted friend and move on with Christ. I do this often.

> "The solo effort to avoid temptation can so exhaust us that we actually make ourselves more susceptible to sin."

Here's an example of how this plays out practically. I've walked down a beach where beautiful women were sunning themselves. They are distracting, yes, but not a source of sin. The women weren't evil or bad. After all, men have the ability to get intrigued even by a woman wearing a full-length gunnysack! The way I respond to this visual temptation is by acknowledging to God the beauty of His creation without pausing to lust, and then I move on with Christ. God can handle honest conversation about real temptation.

Satan is cruel; he takes no prisoners. He tries to destroy everyone he can. He even goes after children. He's relentless in our most discouraging moments. But Jesus has defeated his end game. If you're carrying a heavy burden of sin because of temptation, give it to Jesus; He wants to take the meaning of 'Best Friend' to a whole new level. Then you can walk in the peace of knowing that He loves you, understands your temptations and has secured your victory through the cross.

BEEN GRIEVING?

Have you ever wondered how the body can produce so many tears? Jesus was grieved, and he definitely shed His share of tears. He cried over the city of Jerusalem and its lost condition (see Luke 19:41). He was in emotional agony on the night of His arrest in the Garden of Gethsemane (Mark 14:34). And in John 11:35 we read simply that, as the result of a friend's death, "Jesus wept." This is the shortest verse in the Bible—and it's a powerful one.

Over the last two years I've learned a bittersweet lesson. For years I felt as though I needed to quickly extricate myself and others from sadness, grief and pain. "Let go and move on" was my motto. I have a low tolerance for discomfort. Because of this, I've too often denied myself, my bride, my children, my colleagues and the thousands of people who've called me their pastor the time to process grief and pain. Grief is a necessary part of healing, a process that acknowledges what has happened and accepts the sadness, anger, loss and pain. It's never pleasant and often seems to take way too much time. But grief is real and healthy. The grieving process is intrinsic to the way God designed us.

> "Talking with God about our grief is like wrapping our hands around a hot mug of our favorite drink on a cold day— it's comforting."

Jesus felt the full range of human emotions, including grief. We can learn from His example of leaning into the Father during the hard times. Here's what Jesus prayed in Gethsemane during the most difficult time of His life: "*Abba*, Father, all things are possible for you. Remove this cup from me. Yet not what I will, but what you will" (Mark 14:36). Just as Jesus did, we need to acknowledge our pain and then lean on the Father to get us through it. Talking with God about our grief is like wrapping our hands around a hot mug of our favorite drink on a cold day—it's comforting.

YOU GET ME

The death of the girl I mentioned at the beginning of this chapter radically changed me. Through that experience God gave me eyes to see beyond the way people often appear. How many lives could be helped or saved by knowing the real friendship of Jesus? How many people could have their spirits lifted by knowing that He is not only real but that He understands what we face today? How much thrill could be reclaimed if we were to walk with Jesus in our times of deepest need? Every person alive needs a Best Friend like Jesus.

We all go through ups and downs. Whatever place we're in, from joy and rich relationships to sadness and loneliness, Jesus has been there. He gets us. He understands our every feeling. What comfort to be able to acknowledge "You understand me, Jesus!"

Some of you need to join Jesus in a fresh way on the walk of life. Shut off the cell phone and go for a walk with the One Who wants to walk side by side with you. Listen to His heart. He has more compassion than you can imagine. No matter where you are in life, Jesus wants to come alongside you. He's the One you can turn to in times of celebration and mourning. He loves you so much that He suffered crucifixion — death under the punishing pain of all sin from the past, present and future. Through His sacrifice on the cross you were reconciled with your Heavenly Father. The good news is that Jesus is alive today — and that He wants nothing more than to be your *Best Friend Forever*.

For personal or group study guides and leader support resources, go to www.ThrillOnline.net.

EIGHT

HIGH GROUND

I can keep people defeated with old habits and secret sins.

—Thrill Killer

In the late spring, I used to love driving to a great fishing stream in south-central Alaska. We had to travel down a long, almost impassable road that was a mess during the season we called "Break Up." After the first week of fishing season, mud ruts became a major problem. I'm talking about the kinds of ruts that develop on back roads in cold climates, when the frost comes out of the ground and makes a soupy mush that sucks your vehicle down like quicksand. This road looked like something from an old WWII flick. If you slid into one of those ruts, your rig was an instant mess, and getting out was almost impossible. And if you got high-centered, it would require a bigger rig than yours to get you out.

Over the years we got pretty adept at straddling the ruts and staying on the higher, drier surfaces. But on most trips we'd encounter at least one other rig that had gotten stuck. Sinking into ruts was frustrating, to say the least, but looking ahead to the great fishing kept us coming back down that treacherous stretch year after year.

Whenever I got stuck on that road, I felt pretty stupid. I mean after all, I knew how to drive, and I'd been on this road before. Every time I was determined not to let the mud ruts get me again! But before I knew it, my eyes would wander, or I'd lose concentration and my grip on the steering wheel would ease up. Stink! I'd be stuck again, and I'd have to sheepishly ask the next truck for help — or in my misplaced pride wave it on by.

STUCK AGAIN

Old habits and secret sins are like those mud ruts. We're going along, thinking we have things pretty well under control, when we suddenly find ourselves bogged down in old habits or secret sins — a situation that's spiritually crippling. Thrill Killer wants to get our minds off the greater goal of thrill in Jesus and to waylay us by our spiritual slips into familiar ruts.

We can feel embarrassed when we find ourselves stuck one more time in the same old sin-rut. Sometimes we sheepishly ask God for help, while at other times in our wounded pride we wave Him on by. When I wonder whether God is sick and tired of dragging my sorry tail out of a rut yet again, I remember Thrill Killer's trap. He tells me I'm a failure and that I should keep my eyes pointing down at the mess I've made. He wants me to give up, stop asking for help and just die there in the muck. Thrill Killer's desire is for me to wave off God's offer to extricate me. The sense of shame that comes from repeated failures can keep us stuck in a negative cycle.

I'm sure you can identify. We've all experienced Thrill Killer sucking us down into the ruts on our spiritual road. He wins when he gets us thinking things like: "Mud ruts are just where I belong. I'm always falling in, and asking for help gets old and embarrassing. It's just not worth the effort anymore. Maybe I'm one of those people who's not meant to succeed. I'm not worth helping because I'll just fail again. God's plans are for people who are better than me."

> "We all battle with ruts. Ignoring them just gets us in deeper."

During our spiritual journey, staying on the high ground is a constant challenge, and evil messes with our heads. Here's the thing no one wants to admit: We all battle with ruts. Ignoring them just gets us in deeper. It may feel as though we can't get out or, if we do, that we'll slide right back in soon enough. These are all lies of Thrill Killer.

God has different plans. He wants us to get up out of the muck, get cleaned off and keep our eyes set on Him. To God, each of us is infinitely valuable. He's absolutely in love with us, faults and all. Our past is history, and He has a way of keeping it there! Rising up out of our spiritual ruts and riding on solid, higher ground happens when we converse with God in confession, hear His affirmation of forgiveness and listen as He coaches us forward on the path of life.

CONVICTED

The only time I ever stole anything was one night after church. I went to BI-LO grocery store with a few friends, intending to swipe some grub. The experience was so traumatic I can barely remember the other guys who were with me.

I was scared to death walking into the store. I knew the plan and was prepared, but the prospect of getting caught was excruciating. I had on big, bell-bottomed pants (don't laugh—they were in style at the time!), with cross-country skiing socks underneath. They were the perfect place to hide my stash, and I went for it.

"For being a first-time shoplifter, I was high volume. I shoved Big Buddy bubble gum, Snickers bars, sticks of beef jerky and packs of Kraft cheese and crackers down my socks."

For being a first-time shoplifter, I was high volume. I shoved Big Buddy bubble gum, Snickers bars, sticks of beef jerky and packs of Kraft cheese and crackers down my socks under my pant legs so no one could see my haul. I shuffled through the checkout line pretending I hadn't found what I wanted. Pure adrenaline pumped through my veins.

I got out the door and scooted around the corner. Under cover of darkness I showed my loot to my friends and started munching on some cheese and crackers. Guilt instantly overwhelmed me. I knew stealing was wrong, and I felt miserable.

I knew what I had to do. I sucked in a big breath, reloaded my socks with everything but the pack of half eaten cheese and crackers, and went back inside. I restocked the shelves with my stolen loot and left empty-footed. On my way out, I smiled at the cashier with the deepest sense of relief and freedom. I still owe BI-LO for the cheese and crackers, but they've since gone out of business. (If you're the former owner, contact me. I owe you a buck.)

That night at BI-LO, I was willing to sin in order to get what I thought would make me happy. I'd be cool with the guys for taking all the goodies I wanted without paying. Without paying? That's a joke! The moral dilemma and pain I felt that night are the equivalent to what many of us adults feel when we indulge in sinful habits we think will make us happy. But at what cost?

I know what it's like to have old habits keep popping up. When I've tried to cover up secret sin or fallen into an old pattern, it's like sliding into one of those mud ruts on that old road. If I'm not careful, the guilt and shame can make me believe I'm unworthy to call on God, my rescuer and friend.

Your mud rut probably isn't stealing junk food, but you know what it is. It could be that you're in danger of losing your family or something else of great value because of it. Maybe you're continuously being sucked into old habits and can't seem to get any distance from them before they suck you right back in. Let's be honest. These are common battles for everyone. The strongest word of encouragement I can give you is that you're not alone.

So how do we deal with hard-to-shake tendencies and secret sins that keep sidetracking us and stealing our joy? What do we do about these slips that bog down our spirits and leave us stranded again and again? The solution isn't easy, but neither is it what we might expect. It's having a heart-to-heart talk with God and a few trusted friends who can lift us up with truth. Life is a road that shouldn't be traveled alone. Bringing the ugly into the open breaks the hold Thrill Killer gets on us. Verbalizing our need and sharing the story of how we got stuck yet again brings powerful personal relief.

CHEAP THRILLS

A lot of us get confused about what sin is really all about. Originally, sin was an archery term meaning "to miss the mark." The distance between the bull's eye and where the arrow actually hits is the "sin." But allow me to offer a more full-bodied definition.

Sin is more than just missing the mark. It's what happens when we live as though God isn't enough for us. At its core, sin is idolatry. Everything in which we attempt to find life and meaning apart from God is a substitute. The corporate ladders we climb offer new definitions of success. The ball teams for which we play or cheer, the men or women we date, and our fantasies all become new ways of seeking fulfillment. All of these can become God-substitutes that channel our attention and energy into worshiping the creation over the Creator. They can even begin as good things, designed by God for us to enjoy. Thrill Killer lies to us, suggesting, "You're here to be the most important person you can be. Power, knowledge, money and beauty are the signs that you've really made it. Live for yourself!"

> "Sin is more than just missing the mark. It's what happens when we live as though God isn't enough for us."

This deceptive first step usually goes unnoticed, but it sets us on the path to a toxic future. Pursuing idols becomes the goal of a life lived apart from the God Who created us. Only after our old habits and secret sins have done their damage do we realize how miserably unfit they are to make us truly happy.

One graphic way to explain sin is with the term God used for ancient Israel when his people got stuck in their own ruts. The word is harsh and uncompromising—*adulterers* (see Ezekiel 16). The Israelites chose to make other gods, pleasures and activities their first priority. And God rebuked them. I can just imagine Him saying "You say that you love me, but you're sleeping around with other lovers. You look for pleasure and fulfillment with others and then come home to me. But I still love you."

A good work ethic is an awesome attribute. Family is a gift from God. Sports make for wonderful hobbies. But when these things claim our highest level of attention, energy and affection, we're stepping out on real love for a quick fix that will fade. Spiritual adultery is a brief and costly thrill. The reason God demands our faithfulness is that He knows that only He can provide what we need and desire at the deepest level. God asks for our faithfulness because He loves us and wants our best. Really!

HIGH COST

You know what the problem is with sin? It promises happiness but can't keep its word. Sin is unable to provide the life we so desperately want. To the contrary, it separates us from God. Instead of making us feel content, the aftermath of sin is emptiness.

"You know what the problem is with sin? It promises happiness but can't keep its word."

We can try to comfort ourselves with overindulging, but we'll end up tormented by the consequences of poor health, along with weight and fitness challenges. We can buy a new boat on credit to add fun to our lives, but the budget-crushing debt will likely bring dread instead of relief. Climbing the corporate ladder is great—until a colleague becomes a threat to our next promotion. When we over-commit at work, we may discover too late that it could cost us our families.

In the end, the pursuit of happiness apart from God leads inevitably to negative consequences, as each new thing we consume only whets our appetite for fleeting joy and hollow thrill. Idols will land us in deep mud ruts and will eventually rob us of the thrill we long for. The irony of any sin is that it baits us with independence and freedom but ultimately leads to imprisonment and death. It's like the fable about the trap set with a blood-covered knife. It lured a wolf that licked and licked until his tongue was shredded and he bled to death. Sin and bad habits begin as something in which we indulge, but in the end they devour us.

HIGH ROAD

We can draw encouragement from the story of Moses: "By faith Moses, when he was grown up, refused to be called the son of Pharaoh's daughter" (Hebrews 11:24). Moses was the Jewish baby rescued from the Nile and raised by Pharaoh's daughter. He was brought up among the privileged class of the ancient world, educated in world affairs and trained for military leadership. He was destined for great wealth and powerful influence that even included being the object of worship from the Egyptian people. But Moses walked away from it all! Why?

Because Moses had learned from his early religious upbringing that the One True God honors those who worship only Him. Moses understood at a gut level that all the pleasures in Egypt were short-lived. He didn't know everything that would happen in the future, but he knew enough to cast his lot with God's people.

Radical changes stormed into Moses' life when he secretly murdered an Egyptian soldier for beating a Hebrew slave. His budding leadership skills were derailed by this hidden sin. He wanted to please God by helping his enslaved brethren, but he made the mistake of taking matters into his own hands. Little did he know that his extraordinary training as one of the greatest leaders in history would begin only years *after* his sin had been exposed.

When Moses' short-fused temper led to murder, which he soon enough discovered had not gone unwitnessed, he began his life in exile. Through 40 long years away from his people, caring for sheep, inhaling the sand of desert storms and coming to peace in the presence of God, Moses learned the truth: There's nothing more thrilling or fulfilling than a deep connection with God, coupled with the knowledge that God is pleased with our life.

POOR RETURN

Sin can never provide long-term fulfillment and joy. It ultimately destroys those things that are of most value to us. The coaxing of Thrill Killer causes us to do things that earlier in our lives might have shocked us. I've had one close friend whose life was shattered by a sexual affair. There was a time when he would never have imagined following through on his lust, but the crippling combination of marital disappointment, self-pity and opportunity were all he needed to get sucked into a rut of deadly sin.

Every man and woman who struggles with temptation could tell you that flirting with sin always produces a desire for more of the same because it yields diminishing returns. After a while, the sin that once satisfied us loses its luster. We feel the need to ramp it up, to hit the thrill button a little harder, but we're only digging a deeper ditch. Thrill

> "...sin always produces a desire for more of the same because it yields diminishing returns."

Killer baits us to move past the fantasies of the mind to enactment. But the return on the investment always comes back worth-less. Be aware; sin's appetite is insatiable.

The good news is that Jesus Christ can totally destroy Thrill Killer's plans to ruin our families and our futures. Jesus offers new beginnings and second chances. His forgiveness clears the past so that the future can be wholesome and exciting. Far from beating us up, God restores us to Himself in love. By the grace of God, my friend's marriage survived his affair. Today he shares his story so that good can come from it.

Our God is in the business of redeeming our messes.

"HELL, NO!"

I once asked a friend whether he liked the life he had made for himself. "Hell no," he responded with his head in his hands. The good news is that God offers real life, even while we run from Him: "I spread out my hands all the day to a rebellious people, who walk in a way that is not good, following their own devices" (Isaiah 65:2). We have only to grab God's hands and discover the thrill that can connect us with Him.

In His radical love, God passionately desires to liberate us from our rebellious selves. Like my friend, we can find no better condition for our hearts than by admitting "Hell, no! I don't like what I've made for myself at all." From that truth we can move into a healing relationship with God that begins with forgiveness, both of our past wrongs and of our current sins. This experience of self-awareness and the accompanying pain that drops us to our knees whets our appetites with the first taste of thrill.

God's love for us allows us to be broken down and then spiritually rebuilt, much as a loving dad and mom carefully allow their child to hit the floor while taking his first steps. These parents know the tumbles are coming, but they also know the child will learn to walk through the process. Similarly, God allows us to fall flat so we can look to Him for our next step.

Does God really love us? Oh, baby! You bet He does. Lost, hurting and non-God-seeking people matter to Him (see Luke 19:10). Liars, cheaters, gossips, promiscuous heterosexuals, sexually-active homosexuals, thieves, murderers, haters—God loves 'em all! He wants a friendship with us that's intimate and powerful. You may be "livin' like hell," but that doesn't stop God from valuing you and wanting to lead you to true happiness in Himself.

MIRACLES AND MASQUERADES

I love the honesty of some parolees I've met. I've taken more than one ankle-monitored friend to lunch. I'll never forget sitting down at a bistro in Anchorage with an overly animated man who had a sorry life story. It wasn't pretty. Drugs, infidelity and forgery...he threw it all out on the table. There's something about open people that makes you feel safe in opening up yourself. So I tossed all my own trash into the mix. Before long I began telling him about the power of God to change us. And wouldn't you know it—God touched my friend's heart then and there and performed a miracle. God revealed to him that he was a man in deep need of help, a man who had no way out of his mess unless God changed him.

Today, many years later, my friend still struggles with relinquishing control. He hasn't fully surrendered—yet. I love this man and talk with him occasionally, and am convinced that's God not finished with him. He's up and down, but here's what I've learned about this guy, myself—and probably you. We're better at masquerading and self-managing than we are at actually confessing our need for help.

Thrill Killer insists that the cost of honesty and surrender is too high, cautioning us with words like "Giving yourself completely to God is throwing away any chance for thrill." He wants us to settle for the fleeting moments of cheap fun we can create for ourselves. Thrill Killer will permit us to toggle back and forth between sinning and small personal victories that allow us to breathe a sigh of relief before returning to whatever is causing our pain and defeat—starting the frustrating cycle over, and over, again.

KING-SIZED CLEANUP
My favorite king in the Bible is a young man named Josiah. Josiah became the king of Israel at the age of eight. He came to power on the heels of two wicked kings—his dad, Amon, and granddad, Manasseh—both of whom had prostituted the country to false gods. Israel had been whoring around on God for so long that all copies of the Scriptures had been lost for centuries.

Josiah faced a major fork in the road. Would he continue to sell out the nation or would he return to the one true God? He didn't have a roadmap to lead Israel back to God, but he did have a heart for God. "For in the eighth year of his reign, while he was yet a boy, [Josiah] began to seek the God of David his father, and in the twelfth year he began to purge Judah and Jerusalem of the high places, the Asherim, and the carved and the metal images" (2 Chronicles 34:3).

Faced with a corrupt culture and a kingdom mired in destructive habits and deadly sin, the young Josiah rose to the occasion. His bold and courageous moves to restore the ways of God eventually led the entire nation into incredible blessing and the thrill of walking in relationship with God. Like Josiah, if you've got a heart for God, you've got all you need to pull out of your ruts. If you follow Josiah's example, you will make it to higher ground.

EXTREME MEASURES

Jesus warns that some habits and sins require extreme measures. When speaking of sexual sin and lust, He says, "If your right eye causes you to sin, tear it out and throw it away. For it is better that you lose one of your members than that your whole body be thrown into hell. And if your right hand causes you to sin, cut it off and throw it away. For it is better that you lose one of your members than that your whole body go into hell" (Matthew 5:29–30). Obviously, Jesus is using hyperbole. His goal is to help people break free from the stranglehold of sexual sin. But the principle applies to every area of sin in our lives. The solution to habitual sin is taking radical and extreme measures to deal with it.

Today, in the context of lust and pornography, that may mean making full disclosure to friends or loved ones regarding our sins, loading a software program that blocks porn sites, giving our passwords to a trusted friend or getting rid of our Internet connection altogether.

In the context of money-driven idolatry, that may mean finding another job that pays less money but enables us to be the spouse and parent God has called us to be.

In the context of substance abuse, that may mean admitting our problem and checking into a rehab center to get cleaned up.

If we're a habitual liar, exaggerator or gossip, we may want to write down the names of all the people we've offended and make a point of asking their forgiveness.

All these things, and many more, are serious, life-changing steps that are scary but necessary in order to root out the sin from our soul. They're extreme measures, yes. No matter what ditch we've fallen into, the first thing we need to do is get serious about our sin and do all we can to deal with its sources.

I guarantee that if you get your heart right before God and seriously deal with your sin, He'll renew you, strengthen you and clean you up into a brand new person.

AMAZING LOVE

God knows the details of our lives. That means *every* detail. Do you take comfort in that? Or does it make you cringe? Thrill Killer loves to sell us this lie: "Because God knows your deepest secrets He's angry with you, just chafing to lash out with punishment. God is just waiting for you to step out of line so that He can pop you one." That's the sorry way some humans treat each other—but hardly the caring way in which God, Who is truly good, deals with us. His discipline comes from a heart of love, and it's designed to pick us up and get us moving in the right direction.

> "God knows the details of our lives. That means *every* detail. Do you take comfort in that? Or does it make you cringe?"

The God of the Scriptures is first and foremost a redeemer, not a condemner. As Paul writes, "There is therefore now no condemnation for those who are in Christ

Jesus" (Romans 8:1). That's a fact. As long as we're breathing, there's hope for us in Jesus to be liberated from our sin. That's the way our God operates.

I get frustrated when I hear people preach Thrill Killer's message that God is just looking for ways to smoke us. This polluted message describes God as one who is quick to condemn and punish. The truth is that God begins to extend mercy long before He reaches the first step of discipline. If He didn't, none of us would have made it past "the terrible twos"! For those who think God is quick to judge and eager to condemn, let me ask you this: Why did He send His perfect Son to take the punishment for our sin? Our sins required death. God, in His love, placed that condemnation on His sinless Son, Jesus — all because He loved us and desired to mend the rift between ourselves and Him.

In the words of the writer of Hebrews, "Let us then with confidence draw near to the throne of grace, that we may receive mercy and find grace to help in our time of need" (Hebrews 4:16). Get it? God doesn't want to condemn us! He wants us to approach Him boldly and confidently with the truth. Real thrill, genuine confidence and personal fulfillment in Jesus are *available upon request*. Since Jesus knows exactly how we feel and what we need, we'll be amazed at how He goes about transforming us.

Want to see what the heart of Jesus looks like? One description is that of a shepherd who fights off dangerous predatory animals 24/7/365. He leads His sheep to waters that are fresh and pollution free. This shepherd respects our need for rest and safety, and He sets boundaries for our protection, just as we do for our kids. He doesn't allow us to stumble over a cliff; He guards our steps. "When He saw the crowds, he had compassion on them, because they were harassed and helpless, like sheep without a shepherd"

(Matthew 9:36). Thrill Killer wants us to believe that God is totally disinterested in us, but God cares deeply about our helplessness as we wallow in life's struggles!

Recognizing God's help and intervention isn't always easy. So ask Him to make them clear to you. Not only does He want you to see His hand in your life; He also wants to be known by you—because He cares so much.

> **"We fear telling others about our secret sins and noxious habits because we've had those confessions used against us in the past."**

We fear telling others about our secret sins and noxious habits because we've had those confessions used against us in the past. But God sees our pain and is well aware of the ways in which we've been abused, betrayed or hurt. Far from using our sin against us, He'll free us from it. He loves us despite the junk we're lugging around.

"GOD, HELP ME"

Late one night I was doing a training run with a friend's sled dogs and a few guys who were new to the sport. We were in a hurry and were dealing with a green and unruly team of dogs. In the rush to get them hooked up, a dog was put into the team backward by one of the new guys. As I shined my headlamp over the team I was shocked to see two eyes reflecting light back at me. The dog looked scared to death. I think he knew what was about to happen. If we started off without turning him in the right direction, he'd get dragged down the trail. We quickly corrected the situation, and if ever a dog had a look of relief and gratitude, it was this one.

There's a parallel to be shared between my turning around a dog and God turning around a king. Let's return to young King Josiah for a moment. One of the most telling facts about Josiah's reign is that it was only after he'd taken extreme measures to clean up the culture and had set out to rebuild the temple, Israel "coincidentally" rediscovered the long-lost Scriptures. Josiah asked that the sacred books be read aloud to him. When he heard the words of God, he was shattered, realizing how far his nation had strayed from God's teachings. Israel had been headed in the wrong direction for many years. In a desperate expression of the need for God's help, Josiah tore his clothes. In light of the nation's sinful past, he asked some leaders to go and find out just what the future held for Israel.

The men went to a prophetess named Huldah, who conveyed this message for the king: "Because your heart was penitent, and you humbled yourself before the LORD, when you heard how I spoke against this place and against its inhabitants, that they should become a desolation and a curse, and you have torn your clothes and wept before me, I also have heard you, declares the LORD. Therefore, behold, I will gather you to your fathers, and you shall be gathered to your grave in peace, and your eyes shall not see all the disaster that I will bring upon this place" (2 Kings 22:19–20).

Do you know what God desires from us when we're stuck in old habits and secret sin? Truthfulness! And honesty comes when we're awakened by God to see the damaging junk in our lives for what it is. That junk may have started out as cheap thrills or premeditated bad choices, but now it brings us tears of true regret. If this is you, tell God you're sorry for the sins that have hurt yourself and others. Don't hold anything back. Confess all of your hurts and mistakes. Sorrow brings tears for some, and this process may break you down, but God is there to build you up, better and stronger than before.

God promises to accept those who are brokenhearted over their moral, spiritual and financial failures. What a thought! What was once a mess can be made clean and new. God is a turnaround specialist Who guarantees that His results will be beyond anything we could ever have imagined.

> "God is a turnaround specialist Who guarantees that His results will be beyond anything we could ever have imagined."

When we're confronted with the truth, we have a choice to make. Do we wave God off with self-justification or blame-shifting? Or do we flag Him down and welcome His much-needed help? The coolest thing about God is that He lives both on the high ground *and* in the deepest ruts. "For thus says the One who is high and lifted up, who inhabits eternity, whose name is Holy: 'I dwell in the high and holy place, and also with him who is of a contrite and lowly spirit, to revive the spirit of the lowly, and to revive the heart of the contrite'" (Isaiah 57:15).

True desire to change, with God's help, can't be faked. But God will never reject a humble heart, and He'll always meet us where we are (see Psalm 51:17).

LIE DOWN AND LIVE

One day my dad and I were fishing at Ship Creek in downtown Anchorage. The tide was coming in fast, and when the big tides sweep up that river they can change water levels by more than 30 feet within several hours.

We noticed a man fishing out on the mud flats. No one who knows the area goes out there because it's a high-risk gamble when the tide changes. When it came time for him to move to higher ground, he couldn't. His feet were trapped in the mud that was compressed under the massive pressure from the incoming tide. Realizing that he'd missed the signs of danger, this fisherman began struggling to free his feet so that he could run to safety. But the more he struggled, the deeper he sank. Time and again he tried to pull himself out, but the incoming tide was rising so fast he didn't have a chance to save himself. No matter how much energy and strength he exerted, nothing changed. The situation only got worse!

He was going to die— unless someone rescued him. Dad and I weren't willing to leave him trapped in that sucking mud. After managing to get a rope out to him, we gave him clear instructions. In order to be saved, he had to be willing to stretch flat out on the muddy surface and let

> "He was going to die—unless someone rescued him. Dad and I weren't willing to leave him trapped in that sucking mud."

us do all the work. This seemed risky and counterintuitive. He had to trust us and resist his natural desire to keep struggling. He had to allow us to fight for him. He finally gave in and allowed us to pull him to safety.

Battles with sin are very much like that. We have to look at our situation, see its deadly outcome and ask some hard questions, like:

How did I get into this mess?

Do I want out of this sin?

Did it work the last time I tried to free myself?

The toughest thing about dealing with secret sin and nonproductive habits is laying out the whole ugly truth to

God and trusting Him to save us. No games, no blaming, no dressing up the truth. God already knows our truth— and He knows we can't save ourselves.

Life change happens when we own up and let God save us. We've got to acknowledge the gunk of our sin and quit the pride fight. Only then will we see God do what He does best—drag us to safety out of Thrill Killer's trap.

The reality of God's kingdom is that He has already done the work of salvation we so desperately need. Just as with those mud ruts that sucked me in on my way to the fishing hole, the only way out of our sin and hurtful habits is to let God pull us out. Just as was the case with the guy trapped on the mud flats, there's not a thing we can do to better our situation. And you know what? That's the most refreshing part of it all! All we can do is rest in God, stop struggling and let Him pull us to high ground.

In his letter to the Romans Paul writes, "When you were slaves to sin, you were free in regard to righteousness" (6:20). He's saying that we can't live a righteous life on our own. "But," Paul continues, "What fruit were you getting at that time from the things of which you are now ashamed? The end of those things is death. But now that you have been set free from sin and have become slaves of God, the fruit you get leads to sanctification and its end, eternal life" (vv. 21–22). What exactly does this mean?

It means that we've been given a new life of spiritual victory. God is there for us. He isn't finished with us. When Israel gave up on God, He didn't give up on his people but kept on extending His mercy. He hasn't given up on us either. Don't make the mistake of neglecting the liberty that *is* ours (not that could or might be ours) through Christ. He can free us from the power of sin and give us a new life. But we first have to trust Him.

God's way always leads to higher ground. Yes, this new life has huge implications for eternity, but it also has consequences for today. We don't have to be stuck in a rut. God can free us from Thrill Killer's muddy grip.

Go for the high ground!

For personal or group study guides and leader support resources, go to www.ThrillOnline.net.

NINE

PUBLIC INTOXICATION

I get people working hard at looking good.

—Thrill Killer

Bondo is a kind of putty that can be molded into pretty much anything and then sanded smooth. It's in high demand in Wasilla, Alaska, where I lived for two years. When you combine icy roads with high school drivers, the result can be some pretty banged-up vehicles.

Some guys used Bondo like old pros. The goal was to apply a coat of paint to the car or truck without the Bondo-repaired area showing. If this were done right, you couldn't see that the car had been wrecked only a few weeks earlier. We learned the hard way to carry a magnet when buying a used vehicle. The magnet clamped tight to any metal, but its failure to stick was a telltale sign that Bondo lay beneath the glossy finish. If you weren't careful, you'd buy a car that looked great but was damaged and had been made to look good with Bondo. I had more than one friend whose "new" truck hit a pothole, only to have a Bondo chunk fall out and expose the ugly truth…a messed-up vehicle that still needed work.

Spiritually speaking, we're all born dinged up. Our sin, as well as the sins of others, mars our lives and leaves us in need of repair. We often choose a shortcut instead of the needed repair job and smooth in layers of spiritual Bondo to hide our gouges, hoping our dents and blemishes won't be too noticeable. But when we hit challenges, our spiritual Bondo cracks loose, and our dents are revealed.

When this happens, there's no more pretending. We'll either admit our need for quality repair work or we'll try more quick fixes until we end up in the spiritual wrecking yard. Genuine thrill begins to build when we finally admit we're fixer-uppers that need to go straight to the expert on spiritual restoration—Jesus. The only real fix is for us to allow Him to do His work—cleaning out all the filler in every crevice, pulling the frame into alignment, tapping out the metal to where it belongs, and prepping the surface for a new coat of paint. It takes time, expertise, diligence and patience, mixed with some pain, to restore us. But when the job is done, the results are awesome!

BONDO SPIRITUALITY

Problems inevitably surface when we perform and try to impress. Having a good idea of how we should look on the outside but trying to achieve it in deceptive ways is a classic ploy of Thrill Killer. Thrill Killer assures us that quick fixes are easier than real fixes. Evil tempts us to cover up our flaws and then mocks us for being a pretender. Spiritual-performance Christianity grinds on us. We get the feeling that things just aren't right. Going through the motions leaves us empty and in a tough spot. Most of us know what we want our lives with God to look like—inner peace, future hope, healing for hurts and release from the bondage of sin and addiction. But without a real work of grace, we're left with fake and flimsy substitutes.

Jesus made the analogy that people who fake being right with God are like cups that appear clean on the outside but on the inside are crusty with old food bits and backwash (see Matthew 23:25). *Nasty* is the word that describes the hypocrisy of trying to look good on the outside, knowing full well that none of it is real on the inside. This is called performance, and the truth is that pretending to have the real thing with God is worse than living authentically without Him. The pain **"...pretending to have the real thing with God is worse than living authentically without Him."** of this kind of existence would be crushing if not for the hope that the ultimate restorer of thrill, Jesus, doesn't intend to leave us in this hypocritical situation.

OFF THE HOOK

There are a myriad of half measures and quick fixes that do nothing to change human nature. Thrill Killer encourages us to take the self-help way. When Bondo becomes part of our spiritual repair kit, we've set ourselves up for Thrill Killer's taunts. He whispers, "You can never expect full restoration, and hiding your dents is your only alternative." Or he invites, "Keep working it. You just need more spiritual elbow grease." So we learn to carry an emergency kit, just in case we need a little touchup.

The good news is that we aren't lost causes. There's hope for us in Jesus. He calls out to us, "I'm real, and I can transform all that you are into someone new. I can put you to mint condition. You're off the hook—no more pretending. This is my job, and I'm going to complete it."

When we give up on our fake life and ask Christ to make us new, we know for certain that it's all about Him and not about us! A thrilling sense of freedom begins to envelop us as we realize that through Jesus all of our sins (dents) are forgiven. Deep down, we know we can't do this ourselves. As a result, a genuine thanksgiving to God wells up within us. We're pumped about our new life. Praising Him is what we were created to do. Connecting our souls to God brings daily joy. Our hope is grounded in Him and in His work in us.

Still, a word of caution is in order for all believers. The work of forgiveness and healing that Jesus does in us can make us think that *we* had better get busy being "Christian." We may think it's our job to stay on God's good side. We want our lives to reflect that God has done something for us, and we can start responding in terms of those downers I refer to as "should dos." We can slip into a mindset of personal effort.

Nothing could be more devastating because this type of thinking derails the thankful heart from praising God. Zeroing in on "should dos" puts the focus on ourselves; if we feel we're doing well, we'll give ourselves a pat on the back! And that's exactly what Thrill Killer is after. He works hard to get us working harder at looking good.

But ultimately we can't do it. We spin our wheels and slather on the Bondo to hide what only God is able to repair. This common problem comes in part from a Westernized mindset that idolizes rugged individualism. I cheer individual uniqueness—and God does too—but only when we're walking in His power. Standing alone and working independently of God will ruin any possibility of thrill.

FUTILE EFFORTS

I've seen this in my own life. A lesson I've learned the hard way is that self-will is powerless to make me a great dad, husband or leader. I've tried to do the right thing in my own strength, only to be burdened by the strain of the wasted effort. The irony about trying to do it all on my own is that any level of victory I achieve is shallow. Fake love, false peace and fleeting joy are all indicative of living apart from God. My self-willed attempts to make my life fulfilling brings hollowness instead. And working hard to do right in my own power only distances me from God's power.

The futility of self-effort is described in Galatians 5:4-5: "You are severed from Christ, you who would be justified by the law; you have fallen away from grace." Paul identifies human effort (the law) as a joy-and-grace-killer. He knew that a list of humanly devised rules would never help the people he cared for. They needed the grace and power of God flowing into and out of their hearts. Because Paul had spent much of his life as a Pharisee, trying to earn God's favor under the law, he knew the pointlessness of trying to do so — and he had since that time discovered the power of grace in Christ (see Philippians 3:3-11).

All of this self-effort just sets us up for another crash. Attempting to be good in our own strength is like trying to keep God's law. We can't possibly do it, and our attempt to do so results in spiritual frustration and alienation from Jesus. He seems distant, which causes us to become even more discouraged. Self-will initiates a spiritual freefall that hurls us farther from the source of life. Sadly, that's the way it works. The harder we try to be good in our own efforts, the farther away God seems. We actually fall away from the power source that transformed us. Our striving damages our connection with God.

FIRM FAITH

I was recently watching a popular awards show on TV. The host was one of the most foul-mouthed jerks I've ever seen. His derision of women (he actually stated that he wanted to have sex with one particular woman he pointed at), his cheap shots at popular young talents who dared to call themselves Christians, and his graphic description of bisexual lust made me sick. In my own strength, I imagined this guy as the enemy—someone I wanted to see lose. I could envision myself sprinting onto the stage and taking him down in defense of my country, female virtue and everything wholesome. I'm not kidding! This creep ticked me off so much that every muscle in my body was clenched tight.

Our real character is revealed in the face of conflict. It's much easier to look good in the "no conflict" zone in which everybody agrees with us. But when challenged by someone who champions a value system that seeks to trash our own, or when injustice thrives, our emotions can blow wide open. Our true character is exposed.

When conflict arises, when injustice occurs or when our pride is hurt, that's when we get a glimpse of what we're really made of. That's when the spiritual Bondo breaks loose. Our dents, scratches and dings are all exposed. What we need is faith. Without authentic faith we're so desperate to look right that we settle for putty when our Maker could put us in mint condition. "And without faith it is impossible to please him, for whoever would draw near to God must believe that he exists and that he rewards those who seek him" (Hebrews 11:6). God's reward is full renovation for those who seek Him.

BORN CONSUMERS

There's only one drive that outweighs our desire to create something of worth—our drive to consume. We're born to consume. And every day we have the chance to choose what we're going to consume. Freedom of choice is something God gives us. In our own power and left to our own devices, we tend to focus on what we *shouldn't* consume rather than what we *should*.

> "There's only one drive that outweighs our desire to create something of worth—our drive to consume."

I was raised in a church culture that championed getting away from sin and avoiding certain temptations. That's a good goal, but achieving it is beyond our ability. In my church culture, the measure of one's spiritual health was often based on those things to which one said no. Having our lives buttoned down and in order was the hook. The bait was approval. So we said no to the bad stuff—like drugs, pornography, pride, gossip, alcohol and many other enticements that are truly destructive.

But problems always arise when our lives are marked by pride in what we *don't* do. This is a dangerous condition because we create the perception that the Christian life is defined by the bad stuff we avoid instead of by the thrill of being immersed in God. This deadly thinking shifts our focus to fearing destructive things rather than living in the power, victory, fullness and thrill that can be ours as consumers of what God has for us.

The power of self-will failed me, and I suspect it has failed you as well. The more I tried to fix my life in my own strength, the more miserably I failed, all the while pretending that everything was just fine. But as I slowly learned to trust God with my "No" list, I began to notice that the more I focused on Him in everyday life the less significant my temptations seemed. I've found that the secret is daily plugging *in to* God, not focusing on rooting stuff *out of* my life. The answer for any destructive behavior is not self-will—it's a life given over to God, a life of trusting Him to change us!

Christians known for being anti-this and anti-that are a sickening representation of Jesus. Our friends, neighbors and kids need to see kindhearted actions from clean-hearted people who are big-time consumers of God—people who produce eye-catching, mouth-watering fruit that emanates from the Spirit of God. This kind of fruit results from being intoxicated with God.

SPIRITUALLY INTOXICATED

Paul expressed it this way: "And do not get drunk with wine, for that is debauchery, but be filled with the Spirit" (Ephesians 5:18). This passage has almost nothing to do with consuming alcohol and everything to do with consuming God. Paul instructs us to be filled with God to the point that He intoxicates us. Too much wine slurs our speech and causes us to act foolish, but drinking in more of God will sweeten our speech and cause us to act godly. Talk about heady!

The great thing is that God and His word constantly call us to the bigger yes rather than to no. Being intoxicated by God's Spirit allows us to experience and express a thrill that comes from something out of this world—literally. Being publicly intoxicated by the Spirit of God radiates something greater than a moral or sober life. It reveals an extraordinary life that is both uncommon and exhilarating.

NEW WINE

When our focus is on the things we *shouldn't* do, there's no thrill in the things we *can* do in God. When our eyes are fixed on the "shouldn'ts," rest assured we'll be caught in a self-willed spiral of sin—falling and repenting again and again instead of experiencing victory over sin.

For those of us who are, or will be, parents, the best measure of great kids isn't their avoidance of alcohol, drugs and sex but their intoxication with God's love, power and fullness. An understanding of God's love for us leads to this spiritual intoxication. We're faced with a choice: We can either raise our kids to duke it out in their own strength and try to look good by saying no to sin, or we can raise kids who are so blown away by God's greatness and goodness that they have no desire to sin against Him.

DARE TO DESIRE

There's a great book by John Eldredge titled *The Journey of Desire: Searching for the Life We Only Dreamed Of.* In it the author describes our need to consume God: "This may come as a surprise. Christianity is not an invitation to become a moral person. It is not a program for getting us in line or for reforming society. It has a powerful effect upon our lives, but when transformation comes, it is always the after effect of something else. Something at the level of our hearts. At its core, Christianity begins with an invitation to desire." Authentic faith that thrills recognizes that we're born with appetites and with an innate capacity to consume.

"This may come as a surprise. Christianity is not an invitation to become a moral person."

Some of you have wondered, "How can I desire to enjoy God?" My response is *How can you* not *desire to enjoy God?* George Mueller was a man of modest means who nonetheless left an enduring legacy. He built orphanages where, based on the channel of prayer, God provided for the sustenance of thousands of rescued children. Mueller's legacy of trusting in Christ continues through these orphanages today.

Listen to what George Mueller said: "The first great business to which I attend every day is to have my soul happy in the Lord." He goes on to say, "Before I go to work and do the business of the church or preach a message, the first and greatest business of the day is to have my soul happy in Jesus." *Boom!* That's exactly what we're called to do—to have our souls happy in God. We need to head out in the morning filled up with God. Then, as we see legalism or self-will trying to alter our view of God, we can recognize Thrill Killer trying to mess with our minds.

DRINK IT UP

The obvious question becomes *How do we consume God?* We make it so hard at times, but that need not be. Let me illustrate.

When God transformed me in 1984, I was quite the party animal. I'd consumed so much beer and hard stuff that I haven't felt the need to drink in a couple decades. I truly consumed my lifetime quota in just a few short years. But I'm occasionally around people who drink, and I've observed something common to all cultures—people get drunk. This was true in Paul's time too, and he used it as a metaphor that people recognized then and that we understand now. He likened the way people get drunk with wine to the way we can get intoxicated with the Spirit.

There's no mystery to being drunk with the Spirit. It's this simple: Instead of turning to God-substitutes such as alcohol, drugs, materialism or pride to fill the emptiness inside, we turn to God to fill us up. Doing this is as easy as choosing the Holy Spirit and asking Him to partner with us. We intentionally spend time seeking Him in prayer and meditation. And we linger. This isn't a quick process, but our desire to consume God can bring satisfaction that nothing else can. The most important role of the Holy Spirit is to guide us into all truth (see John 16:13). This is why God is able to do what we can't. Only He can guide us and direct our choices into the path of thrill. If we want the truth, a renewed life and the power to walk in it, we need His Spirit.

One of the problems with us Americans is that we're in too much of a hurry. It's in our cultural blood. We subscribe to TiVo so we can skip the commercials and watch our shows faster. We eat fast food. We speed boost our broadband Internet. We skim our e-mail, and we text so we don't have to verbally connect—it takes too much time! We do all this so we can get on to the next thing. But what are we missing at this pace?

DEEP DRINK

I don't know about you, but I'm tired of all this hurrying! I want my life to be a reflection of the Holy Spirit quietly intoxicating me. I want to drink deeply of His gifts of love, joy, peace, self-control and so much more. My desire is to quit performing and start trusting that God will do what He's promised.

Right now, ask God to give you a strong shot of His Holy Spirit. He will. Only the Spirit can initiate change in our behavior. He brings us incredible comfort and power. Invite Him, "I want to be known as a person who is full of You, a person who has something to offer others. Fill me, God!"

The great thing about being filled with the Spirit is that we can tap into His power at any time and in any place: in a meeting, in the midst of a conflict with a spouse, during fierce temptation, interacting with people who don't have a relationship with God — in virtually any situation in which we might find ourselves. The key is to continually drink in the Spirit. As Paul instructs us, "Rejoice always, pray without ceasing, give thanks in all circumstances; for this is the will of God in Christ Jesus for you. Do not quench the Spirit" (1 Thessalonians 5:16–19). Continuously drinking in the Spirit breaks us of the notion that only certain times are appropriate for paying attention to God — like during devotions, at mealtime or in our bedtime prayers. It reminds us that in all times and circumstances God is there to be sought and found.

> "Authentic followers of Christ drink up the Holy Spirit whenever possible."

If you listen closely, you'll hear the Holy Spirit's assurance that "I never run out of what you need. I know your challenges. I love you, and I'll fill you." Every one of us faces tough choices every day. God is offering us the opportunity to choose Him and reject the God-substitutes of today's world.

Authentic followers of Christ drink up the Holy Spirit whenever possible. Our children, grandchildren, spouses, friends and communities need us to be people who raise high a toast to the Living God.

WE CAN'T—GOD CAN

Jesus provided us with a vision of a radically different existence, asking, "For if you love those who love you, what reward do you have? Do not even the tax collectors do the same? And if you greet only your brothers, what more are you doing than others? Do not even the Gentiles do the same? You therefore must be perfect, as your heavenly Father is perfect" (Matthew 5:46–48). Perfect? God wants us to be perfect? You've gotta be kidding! "No," Jesus responds, "I'm not kidding. And I've provided a way." The kicker is that He calls us to live perfectly, all the while knowing *we* can't do it.

There are a couple of key truths that are bedrock to the balance of this chapter. First, *it's all about Him*. It always has been, and it always will be. The problem with the Bondo-patched life is that it's all about us trying to live by our own strength. Instead, we need to realize that it's God who works in us — and that what He's started He wants to finish. As Paul writes, "I thank God in all my remembrance of you, always in every prayer of mine for you all making my prayer with joy, because of your partnership in the gospel from the first day until now. *And I am sure of this, that he who began a good work in you will bring it to completion at the day of Jesus Christ*" (Philippians 1:4–6, emphasis mine).

Second — and this is no side thought — *every command, request or invitation of God is linked to greater joy and fulfillment in Him*. Whatever He asks of us is always inextricably linked to thrill and to the best life He has to offer. Jesus emphasizes this with these words: "If you keep my commandments, you will abide in my love, just as I have kept my Father's commandments and abide in his love. These things I have spoken to you, that my joy may be in you, and that your joy may be full" (John 15:10–11).

Don't miss the connection. Complete joy is based on responding to the calling, commands and invitation of God. Keep in mind that the promise *is* for joy. Life is hard, and sometimes we don't feel joy; but God is the consummate promise keeper. Joy will be the ultimate and inevitable result of drinking deeply of Him.

SOBER PERSPECTIVE

Here's how this works for me. Remember the crude comedian host who was driving me crazy? God asks me to love this guy. There are a couple things I know to be true. First, that comedian doesn't know God as I do and has yet to be spiritually transformed. He's unable to honor God because he doesn't know Him. The only thing that should amaze me is that this guy isn't doing even crazier things. Without God in our lives, there's no telling how far we can slide. If there's anything good at all in me, it's only because of God, "For it is God who works in you, both to will and to work for his good pleasure" (Philippians 2:13).

Second, there's only one way for this guy to come to know God, and it isn't through condemnation but through someone genuinely caring for his soul. No, I don't have to approve of his antics—in fact, I'm still ticked off about them—but I can choose to display radical love if I want him to know the real Jesus. In this instance, since I can't relate to him personally, that means prayer. Prayer moves the hand of God (2 Chronicles 33:13). I doubt I'll ever have the privilege of directly talking with the comedian who essentially spit on all women and mocked Christ-followers. But I don't doubt that God loves him and may move someone into his path as He pursues this guy. Asking God to reveal Himself to this lost man is my sacrificial act of kindness. It's evidence of my intoxication with God.

Most transformed people have a clear understanding of what authentic faith should look like. We find the thrill of authentic faith only when we shift our focus from our own efforts. Our attempt to produce good fruit by self-will only leads to frustration. I can keep it real only so long as Jesus is working through — and sometimes in spite of — me. When we stop performing or trying to fix ourselves, we allow God to use us as conduits of His power. The more fully we surrender to God and His work, the more we open ourselves up to receive from Him and to pass along to others what we've received.

VINE TIME

Jesus uses a metaphor that classically describes how we are to position ourselves in order to consume God: "I am the vine; you are the branches. Whoever abides in me and I in him, he it is that bears much fruit, for apart from me you can do nothing.... [B]y this my Father is glorified, that you bear much fruit and so prove to be my disciples" (John 15:5, 8). God smiles when we display authentic faith in abundant ways. One of the best ways for us to give God glory is to bear good fruit. The way we produce fruit is to get grafted into the True Vine.

Jesus uses the metaphor of producing fruit to describe what our lives as Christ-followers are to look like. And Paul enumerates this fruit as "Love, joy, peace, patience, kindness, goodness, faithfulness, gentleness, [and] self-control" (Galatians 5:22). Character like this — God stuff, as I like to call it — is out of this world.

Authentic faith is so radically different from what we would naturally expect. Just check out the Beatitudes in Matthew 5. Who is blessed in the kingdom of God? Those who have a realistic view of themselves and a high view of God are the ones who exhibit true faith. Our positioning is everything. We realize the power of God when our own performance is cancelled. When we acknowledge that God is God and we're not. When I am the conduit and He is the current, God's fruit grows easily because His life is flowing through me.

> "Fruit doesn't grow from our efforts *for* God but rather from our resting in God."

The metaphor of the vine and the branches illustrates proximity to Jesus as the most powerful of all positions. The interesting thing about a branch is that it has nothing to offer on its own. A branch can produce nothing if it's disconnected from the vine. We must let Jesus produce fruit in us. Fruit doesn't grow from our efforts *for* God but rather from our resting *in* God.

PROXIMITY, NOT PERFORMANCE

Amazingly, our need for rest is the reason God designed the Sabbath. Sabbath is more than a day of resting from work; it's a day of resting in—and *into*—God. Proximity to Jesus requires spiritual discipline. Cheerful quiet, peaceful solitude, meditation on God's Word and character, consideration of God's creation and contemplative prayer are just a few of the disciplines I use to rest into God. It actually works, and engaging in these activities makes for a huge mental and behavioral shift in my mind and heart. Getting our mindsets as individuals and churches off *performance* and onto *proximity* is a shift that needs to occur, and when it does the thrill becomes a reality. At the end of the day, it's a matter of focus.

When we focus on proximity to Christ, we won't be distracted by analysis of our fruit production. Our full attention will be on Jesus. Conversely, whenever we try to measure our own performance and level of fruit production, we take our eyes off Jesus and lose our connection with Him. Staying close and committing to personal proximity to Jesus is the answer—just as, in real estate, it's all about location, location, location.

There's absolutely nothing as spiritually heady as bearing authentic fruit. Humbly observing what God has done, without being enamored with it, is critical. Focusing on the fruit Jesus creates in us can cause us to lose focus on Him. And if Thrill Killer can get us to be captivated with the fruit rather than with the vine, he'll soon have us trusting in our own strength and abilities.

I've seen in my own life that trials and pain are gifts from God to pull me back toward—and into—Himself. God can give us extended periods of dryness and frustration with our performance because His passion is for authentic fruit that gives Him glory and gives us joy. Someday when we look around and catch a glimpse of all the fruit that has been produced in our lives without any effort on our part, we'll be shocked, amazed and, yes, thrilled. Better yet, God is pumped to watch our lives produce His fruit. Remember, He wants us to win.

PROXIMITY, BABY

Proximity comes in many forms. Jesus tells a wonderful story in a key passage for all of us struggling to change our performance-based thinking: "And calling to him a child, he put him in the midst of them and said, 'Truly, I say to you, unless you turn and become like children, you will never enter the kingdom of heaven. Whoever humbles himself like this child is the greatest in the kingdom of heaven'" (Matthew 18:2–4).

Jesus scolded the disciples for turning the little children away from Him. He was pleased that the kids just wanted to be near Him. They came up, leaned on him and probably crawled onto his lap. He loved on them like a father, and then He told the adults they needed to become like these little ones. This is awesome and difficult for adults to comprehend. It means that all the over-working, over-thinking and over-strategizing for our own success has got to stop. Christ, and Christ alone, can position us for participation in His best plan for our every endeavor.

I've carried an infant onto a stage before a crowd to illustrate this. The baby watched my mouth when I spoke and listened to my voice, even though she was too young to understand the words. She completely relied on me, trusting my arms to keep her safe. I would never have dropped her. Even though her communication skills were limited, she offered all kinds of valued feedback. Gurgling, cooing and smiling, she conveyed that she had no fear — only trust — and that she wanted to play! This is where God wants me. And it's where He wants you.

> "Go on, be like a little child. Be absolutely dependant. Look to Jesus."

Go on, be like a little child. Be absolutely dependant. Look to Jesus. Fix your eyes solely upon Him. Listen to His words and trust Him. Notice the changes He brings in your thoughts, choices and friendships. Just hang out with Jesus. Proximity is everything. Performance has got to be cancelled. I promise you that becoming intoxicated by Jesus will produce good fruit and transformed behavior. It will give us what we could only have imagined before — the life of thrill. No Bondo required!

The next time you go to a party or have occasion to see someone lit up, let the situation be a trigger in your soul that cries out, "God, intoxicate me with Your Spirit." Public intoxication can actually be a great thing—when you're drinking deeply from God.

This thrill's for you. Cheers!

For personal or group study guides and leader support resources, go to www.ThrillOnline.net.

TEN

ELEVATE

**I want Christ-followers to be intimidated and
discouraged by the world in which they live.**

—Thrill Killer

Thrill Killer wants us to look at the world and complain
"It's going to hell in a handbasket." But hold on here. A
quick glance at our own lives reveals that it's precisely
when we're broken and falling apart that God can do His
greatest work in us.

I'm holding out hope. I believe that a great new awakening could light a fire of spiritual passion in the world,
even in the midst of a bad economy, wars abroad, terrorist
threats and high unemployment. When Jesus pronounced
the poor in spirit to be blessed, He meant that being aware
of our spiritual poverty can ultimately lead to spiritual
prosperity.

With increasing instability, spreading terror and struggling financial markets, we're beginning to see the gods of
this day for what they are—false idols, wholly unable to be
the strength of our lives! But this isn't a time for sorrow. It's

a time to hold out hope that the Savior will rescue broken and hurting people who've been betrayed by their faith in money, stature and many other pitiful gods.

Thrill Killer works overtime to keep hurting and lonely people from hearing about all that Christ has to give them. Thrill Killer's aim in concealing the life and thrill God offers is obvious. If he can keep the hope of Christ a secret, he's won! People aren't nearly as self-sufficient as Thrill Killer wants us to believe. And we as Christians aren't as ill-equipped to help others as he wants us to believe.

THE REAL STORY

Albert Einstein once told a friend, "It is strange to be known so universally and yet to be so lonely." It shouldn't be a surprise that Einstein felt this way, but sometimes I forget that life without God is no life at all. People are dying to know and to be known. They long for the God-shaped void in their hearts to be filled.

"It is strange to be known so universally and yet to be so lonely."

I like to sing along with music, sometimes even country music. And I particularly appreciate a song by Zac Brown from a few years back. It's a good driving tune, and the chorus talks about everything American—fried chicken, cold beer and good fittin' jeans. Now, I don't drink beer anymore because I consumed my entire quota in the early 80s, but I do like fried chicken and a good-fittin' pair of jeans. What's crazy is that I have to remind myself that not everybody who sings that song is really living. Not everybody who looks okay is okay.

Thrill Killer tries to lull me into forgetting that without Christ there can be no lasting thrill. Life is a high-stakes game. Everyone is looking for more than this world can offer. What people need is a long, cool, deep drink of the thrill that can be found only in a relationship with Christ. Something that makes them throw back their heads and roar, "Whoa, *baby!*" This kind of hit can't be derived from a cocktail. I'm talking about the pure water that invigorates and energizes—a drink from the well Jesus said would never run dry (see also Isaiah 41:18).

I appreciate the honesty of a 70s hippie band called *America*. The song, titled "Lonely People," swept the nation when it was released. It struck a chord because everybody faces loneliness at times. And every person without God has to mask the loneliness somehow. Chicken, beer and jeans may feel good, but they can't fill the void in our souls. Loneliness is universal. People down the street, next door and in our own homes are all lonely at times. They need Jesus. Those who dare to hold out an empty cup to Him will find that their needs are met beyond imagination and with an unequalled thrill that completely quenches their soul thirst (see Matthew 10:42).

ELEVATE YOUR GAME

This is the time for thrill. It's also the day to reach people in need. With our world in such disarray, we're poised for great things to happen in the spiritual realm. There's incomprehensible potential for a sustained spiritual awakening in our nation and throughout the world. Many people are willing to listen to the truth, and when we authentically care for them and share our life-changing stories, the thrill of God can touch them too. Spiritual connection can happen, and loneliness can dissipate. But there are obstacles that threaten to paralyze believers and make us ineffective.

I resonate with the encouragement from Jesus' half brother James: "Count it all joy, my brothers, when you meet trials of various kinds, for you know that the testing of your faith produces steadfastness. And let steadfastness have its full effect, that you may be perfect and complete, lacking in nothing" (James 1:2-4).

Let me illustrate how this works. As a sophomore in high school I was a sprinter and long-jumper on the track team. Most sprinters are also long-jumpers because one of the keys to getting distance in a long jump is speed. But one of the first things I learned was that there's more to long-jumping success than speed alone.

At the beginning of the season, the coach didn't speak out for quite some time. He silently observed us for several days of practice. At first we thought he was a little out of touch because he just stood in the infield and watched us running and jumping into the pit. One afternoon as we were getting ready to start our practice jumps, he finally spoke. "Gentlemen, hold on there a second." He grabbed a hurdle from the infield and placed it about five feet from the launch point for the jump.

Looking squarely at us, he yelled, "Come on down! Here we go!" As we glanced at each other, it was obvious we were all thinking the same thing: "Is he trying to kill us? What's he doing?"

"Jump over that thing!" he barked.

He was the coach, so we did as we were told. We ran down the runway again and again. Our main objective at first was to survive. Sometimes we nearly did face plants. But guess what? The coach knew what he was talking about. We got more distance because we listened to him and were willing to take the risk.

We learned an important principle: *If you want to go farther in long-jumping, you've got to go higher.* The same thing is true spiritually. Get this in your heart and head: If you want to go farther in this thrilling adventure with God, if you want to be "complete, lacking in nothing," you've got to elevate your spiritual life and overcome the trials facing you.

God uses obstacles as tools to take us farther than we could ever have gone on our own. He miraculously uses them to help us grow spiritually. When we rise up and overcome trials, we experience more from God and in turn have more to pass along to others. I get amped up just writing about this because of how much liberty comes with hurdling obstacles by God's power.

When we share the hope of Jesus with those around us, we'll encounter every kind of fear and obstacle. Be bold in hurdling the roadblocks Thrill Killer sets up to stop you. There's a big world out there, full of lonely and hurting people waiting to hear about the power, love and thrill Jesus has to offer.

> "God uses obstacles as tools to take us farther than we could ever have gone on our own."

THE HEART OF GOD

Have you ever heard a story that, given just a little more context, finally fits with all you know to be true? Since I was a little guy I'd heard these words of Jesus repeated by preachers: "The harvest is plentiful but the workers are few." They were usually preached to get people saved and into the church. As a young man, the message with which I came away was that people are on a highway to hell and that we have to tell them about Jesus. But that's only part of it. Don't get me wrong: I live to see people transformed by Jesus and love to see them involved in a healthy church. But limiting Jesus' concern to this alone shortchanges the truth.

One of the predominant emotions communicated by Jesus was compassion: "Jesus went throughout all the cities and villages, teaching in their synagogues and proclaiming the gospel of the kingdom and healing every disease and every affliction. *When he saw the crowds, he had compassion for them, because they were harassed and helpless, like sheep without a shepherd.* Then he said to his disciples, 'The harvest is plentiful, but the laborers are few; therefore pray earnestly to the Lord of the harvest to send out laborers into his harvest'" (Matthew 9:35–38, emphasis mine). In this passage we see that Jesus' compassion compelled Him to appeal for prayers that workers would be sent to care for these people. And He's still praying that prayer today. The thrilling news is that you and I are called to be a part of the answer!

> "The harvest fields of God's kingdom aren't divided into good and bad people. They're simply full of people like you and me."

The harvest fields of God's kingdom aren't divided into good and bad people. They're simply full of people like you and me who need to be brought into relationship with the God who heals hearts. People need the reconciling and life-changing power of Jesus. Seeing their lives changed testifies to the fact that Jesus is the solution for every challenge. In a culture that lacks compassion, Christ-followers can showcase God's great love for the world (see Matthew 5:16).

THE POWER OF LOVE

Love is power. It's also the foundation upon which everything else is built. When we truly love people, we find the courage to speak into their lives. With love we're willing to risk sharing our hearts, wiping away others' tears and offering a smile or hug to someone in need. We are always to remember that the love of God is part of Jesus' redeeming work and that God uses us to share it. We're His hands and feet.

My wife's preacher-cousin was assigned to a small, failing church. Some in the denomination wanted to shut it down and sell off the property. Instead, its leaders chose my cousin-in-law, a man born with disabilities, to lead the shrinking congregation. With his speaking difficulties and the tremor in his hands, they didn't think his leadership would amount to much. But they couldn't have foreseen what would actually happen in that struggling church and the surrounding community.

When the power of God's message is delivered through a humble servant, everything changes. Being an excellent communicator, my cousin-in-law provided fresh hope to this congregation. Despite his physical challenges, he preached and led with passion and compassion. The hearts and spirits of the church members began to reflect his powerful humility. They reached out to the needy, offered the hope of Jesus and saw many people made new by the Holy Spirit.

Today that little congregation is living proof of the truth of this verse: "But God chose what is foolish in the world to shame the wise; God chose what is weak in the world to shame the strong" (1 Corinthians 1:27). Its members are making huge strides against Thrill Killer's lies that would deceive believers into thinking small and being quiet. Now this church can't possibly be shut down because it's such an amazing success story. Instead, it's adding services to make room for new people—all because it reached out to the hurting and lonely with the love of Jesus.

The denominational leaders couldn't see beyond my cousin-in-law's tremors and halting speech. They couldn't foresee what would soon draw others into that church and community—an unfailing reliance upon Jesus and a heartfelt humility to serve others.

If we're going God's way, we'll find ourselves in fields of lonely people with the chance to make a difference. And allow me to point out that there's absolutely nothing like joining God in His work in our homes, cities, country and world. There's no greater joy than the exhilaration of observing God using us. If we catch this wave, we're in for the thrill-ride of our lives!

LOVE LANGUAGE

I recently returned from a trip that rocked my world. I've been in some tough places in different countries, but nothing like the Mathare slum in Nairobi, Kenya. Walking among those people broke my heart. I met only a handful of the nearly 300,000 inhabitants who call Mathare home, and I was blown away by the devastating poverty there. On one home visit I met a woman who was raising four children alone. She told me through a translator that her husband had left her for another woman.

She had a look of pain on her face that I'll never forget. She hadn't chosen this life, but this is where she had ended up. A couple of her kids hung on to her, while the others played on a small patch of dirt outside their shanty. There was almost no place to walk because the raw sewage ran freely between the shacks. When I saw a pig nearby with its head buried in the human waste digging for food, I began to dry-heave. The scene was unbearable, and it ripped apart my heart.

My attention was redirected when one of the men with me asked me to pray for this desolate woman and her children. As we all bowed our heads, we recognized what a powerful gift it was to lift up this family to Almighty God. The love we shared with them welled up from deep within our souls, and I believe she understood that we cared and was thankful that we were

> "When I saw a pig nearby with its head buried in the human waste digging for food, I began to dry-heave."

willing to help. I wear a bracelet every day that reminds me of the lessons I learned in Mathare, the greatest of which is that love is a language that translates well into any culture or people group (see John 13:35).

GOD CALLS AUDIBLES

Being used by God requires us to stay flexible. With an ear toward heaven and a heart anticipating great things, we can say "God, I'm yours, and I want to be used by you to reach the world. Direct my steps." This is wise because it's ultimately God who directs our lives according to His game plan. "Come now, you who say, 'Today or tomorrow we will go into such and such a town and spend a year there and trade and make a profit'—yet you do not know what tomorrow will bring. What is your life? For you are a mist that appears for a little time and then vanishes. Instead you ought to say, 'If the Lord wills, we will live and do this or that'" (James 4:13–15).

This truth doesn't call us to take a "let go and let God" approach to life, but it does indicate that there's great thrill in being willing to follow God when He gives us new direction. The best teams in football have highly complex playbooks. Each player is required to memorize them so that when a play is called he knows where to be and what to do. On occasion the quarterback will call an audible because he sees a way to exploit the opposition and gain more yardage. An audible changes everything. The memorized play is out the window. No matter how good the play seemed in the huddle, it's gone.

"If you're ready to share the compassion of God, hang on for the thrill."

God calls audibles too. We can have plans in place, but we need to remain ever alert that at the last moment God can make a change. Here's what we need to do: Make plans—great, audacious plans even—but remain consciously attuned to God. He may go with the set play, or He may ask us to change course. He might move us into the path of someone who needs us when we least expect it. If you're ready to share the compassion of God, hang on for the thrill.

BIG REACH

Spiritual flexibility can result in deep personal joy. A powerful illustration of this truth came for me one night when a man called me in desperation. He'd been livin' like hell for over 60 years, 11 of which he had spent in prison, with 3 in solitary confinement. He had shot heroin and used other drugs and alcohol for most of his life. He also owned a couple of strip clubs. This man was a successful entrepreneur in his own way, but I knew he was in desperate need of God. I assured him that I could see him later that night and advised him that I would bring along my wife. What happened when we arrived was truly awesome. This man was broken and ready for Jesus, and God used Junanne to peel back the layers around his heart. She shared with him that although they'd led radically different lives, she could empathize with the pain he was in. I watched them share a mutual understanding of how desolate you can become when you're desperate to alleviate your pain. My wife had dealt with her own agony in more legally and socially acceptable ways than this man, but the pain they shared was nonetheless comparable.

As Junanne described the anguish of her past, this hurting man began to connect her story with his own. Looking at her, he expressed, "Yes, that's exactly what I'm feeling!" Tears of mingled pain and hope flowed down his face. On his knees, holding his hands in the air, he surrendered his lonely, messed-up life to God. He confessed the sin of running from God and asked for forgiveness. He asked Jesus to become his new leader. This man continues to grow in faith to this day.

Junanne's tender use of godly love language bridged the divide between this hardcore man and the forgiving Savior. Before this awesome night, Junanne and this man had shared almost nothing in common. Now they're sister and brother, sharing the same spiritual Father. Awesome!

It's amazing what can happen when we boldly and compassionately go with God and take His love to the hurting. Lonely people who are at the end of their ropes will often grasp truth and walk forward in spiritual freedom like nothing we've ever before seen. Lives are radically changed and rearranged. Broken hearts are mended.

And lonely souls find peace. Our part in these miracles is speaking the truth in the language of love.

Jesus said, "And you will know the truth, and the truth will set you free" (John 8:32). It's so encouraging to know that we don't have to play games with people. We simply need to present truth in a manner that allows hurting people to trust us and, above all, to trust God. If that truth, presented with love, is received, it frees people like nothing else. We don't have to be concerned about our presentation style. The aspects that count are genuine concern and humility, delivered in whatever manner is most natural for us. Remember and understand that it's the Holy Spirit working through us who changes hearts. Our job is simply to speak the truth of God.

> "Our part in these miracles is speaking the truth in the language of love."

SOUL CARE

We live among people who are engulfed in pain that no medical prescription can fully medicate. I believe that the spiritual/emotional pain in our nation and world is epidemic. Let me ask you several soul-care questions that arise for me from just one day of walking through life....

- Who can heal the heart of a man who has just heard that his bride of seven years has had an affair? Who can bring this couple together and heal their pain, shame and anger? Who can restore intimacy in their marriage for the sake of their little son, who clung to them as they wept and prayed? GOD CAN!
- Who can fill the void of a single woman who has lost her last surviving parent? Who can comfort her

at night when she is susceptible to demeaning accusations from Satan? Who can fill her with love when she longs to be married? GOD CAN!

- Who can comfort the mother who told police last night that she fears for her son's life? Who can heal the heart of her young son, who is so confused and sad that he tells his mom he just wants to die? GOD CAN!
- Who can deliver from alcoholism the woman who lives in secret addiction? Who can help shoulder the pain of the husband who's been married to her for 32 years and doesn't know what to do? GOD CAN!

The hope or demise of our nation is not in health care. Our future, viability and vitality rest in soul-care. Who can care for the vast needs of our people? GOD CAN! And what's best, we are the delivery mechanism. We are the hands and feet of God's love. We are privileged to wipe up tears, hug shoulders, and believe with people for a better spiritual tomorrow. For this there is truly no debate....

"Our future, viability and vitality rest in soul-care."

"But how can people call for help if they don't know who to trust? And how can they know who to trust if they haven't heard of the One who can be trusted? And how can they hear if nobody tells them? And how is anyone going to tell them unless someone is sent to do it? That's why Scripture exclaims, A sight to take your breath away! Grand processions of people telling all the good things of God!" (Romans 10:14–16, The Message).

FRESH STORIES

God knocked me over several years ago with something absolutely unexpected. Reading Acts 26, I caught something simple but profound. Paul presented his life-change story in a courtroom full of hardened military leaders, skeptical priests and even King Agrippa. Paul related his unblemished Jewish heritage, strict upbringing and education, and the fact that in his zeal to persecute Christians he'd imprisoned some and helped put others to death. He confessed that with raging fury he'd entered the synagogues to punish Christians and that he'd tried to get them to blaspheme God.

Then Paul shared how the unbelievable had happened while he was traveling to persecute believers in Damascus. He had encountered the risen Jesus on a dusty road. Paul explained to Agrippa and those others in the courtroom how God had blinded him and then spoken audibly to him, questioning why he was trying to quell a movement of His Spirit. Paul went on to describe how he had gone to the house of a man who had told him the truth about Christ, as well as how God had healed his blindness. It's quite a tale of transformation and faith, which Paul followed up with a passionate appeal to the relevance and power of Christ that had made him a champion of what he had once set out to destroy.

But the best part of this story from my perspective is "hidden" in verse 22 — for all to see. It's often the little nuances in God's Word that teach us the most, and this is a prime example. Paul said something that, if we catch, can change our entire perspective and approach to faith: "I have had God's help to this very day." When we look at the bold and fearless faith of Paul, we can learn something here: Yes, Paul had a story, but he also had a *fresh* story. Paul's power and influence were based on the reality that he expected God to show up in the events of his life on a daily basis! He anticipated and experienced God at work so frequently that he didn't have to reach back to a distant story for evidence of God's power. Looking back no further than that very morning, he could find confirmation of God's miraculous work.

The power of story is widely acknowledged, as it should be, but we have a radical insight from Paul here. The most powerful stories are fresh stories, and fresh stories come from what happens every day. The greatest gift we can give a skeptic is up-to-the-minute evidence of God working in us. Nothing could be more impactful in terms of our children, friends and coworkers than the realization that God is "helping us still." The real evidence of God's hand at work in our lives won't just be heard in our words; it will be seen in our actions—actions that radiate Christ's presence in our lives day after day.

Paul could tell this fresh story for one reason: He was a new man, set free from his past religious performance that had caused the deaths of so many. Because he had been forgiven of his crimes, he breathed in and out the goodness of God. His humility and gratitude for eternal life were byproducts resulting from his brokenness over personal sins. This is the most encouraging and challenging thing I've learned from Paul's life.

> "The greatest gift we can give a skeptic is up-to-the-minute evidence of God working in us."

Fresh stories matter because they're evidence of God's recent, current work in our lives. The dynamism of Paul's faith was grounded in the fact that he expected and witnessed God at work every day.

GOD FIRST

Before we try to help others, we need to ask ourselves, "What evidence is there that Christ is at work in my life right now?" Some of you may desire this fresh, daily work of God but fail to see it in your lives. If you long for it and are wondering what to do, I can assure you that God isn't far away. The Scriptures indicate that the ability to function with God's power and to witness His work simply requires that we seek Him first—that we live with a "God first" approach (see Matthew 6:33). The challenge to put God first is one with which we will always battle and into which God will continuously call us back (see Revelation 2:4–5).

A "God first" approach acknowledges Him as our ultimate authority and the giver of everything good. "God First" is a repeated, daily commitment to lay down all our gifts, talents, hopes and dreams before God and to ask Him to take first place in our lives that day. It recognizes that we are what we are by God's grace.

"God first" claims only the righteousness of Christ; it credits nothing to our own strength or goodness. With this in our hearts and minds, we can ask God to direct the events of each new day in a way that manifests His handiwork. In my experience, this request inevitably results in God showing Himself. It rarely happens in the manner in which I imagined it, but it's always awesome.

I've shared with a lot of folks my true faith transformation story from 1984. It's real, and it's powerful. But that was then and this is now. I don't want to reduce my faith journey to a few big events from the past. The Bible indicates that authentic faith produces daily changes. Thrill Killer loves it when Christ-followers have no recent evidence of God's power in their lives because he knows that makes them feel inadequate and renders their witness impotent. *All of that can change today! Go to God.* Ask Him to show you, today, what to do to bring new vitality and a fresh experience of His power into your life. He'll affirm your desire to please Him, and He'll meet you where you are. Walk in obedience to what He shows you. You can experience fresh evidence of His work in and through you, beginning right now.

A movement of believers who are willing to put God first will generate fresh and convincing stories that exhibit overwhelming personal conviction. There's nothing as contagious as the enthusiasm of someone who has just witnessed God working deeply and personally within his or her own heart and life.

SMALL WORLD AFTER ALL

I was recently writing on my patio when I heard a guy yelling in Mandarin, his native tongue. I turned around to witness him chasing his dog. Then he yelled something that made that dog stop on a dime. It hit me that he was yelling "come here" to his dog in a foreign language. I was blown away. I thought, "That dog knows more Chinese than I do!" Here was a bilingual Labrador, a Chinese man, and me, with my Swedish heritage, all together on a sunny day. What a vivid reminder that it really is "a small world after all."

Some friends and I were messing around with Google Earth a while back and were amazed as we spun the globe and viewed shots of a small town in southern Israel. God struck me with how each of those little homes represented lives. Billions of people across the globe share the identical desire to be loved and renewed. I've traveled to many places, and what's most amazing to me isn't how different we are but rather how similar. We share a universal need to experience the thrill of life. Thrill Killer wants to keep that from ever happening.

There's a big world out there. There are fields of lonely people who are looking for the thrill that only God can give. And those fields aren't necessarily far away. They may well be located right outside our front door. Love transcends language barriers. Behind the accents and cultural differences are millions of people who, whether or not they recognize it, are ready for the truth, liberty and thrill to be found only in God. By now, you know what you need to do. Fall before God and tell Him you're all His. Tell Him you're willing to follow Him. Give Him permission to use your personality, talents and experiences to give you a thrill-filled life, and to let you pass along the thrill to others.

> "Here was a bilingual Labrador, a Chinese man, and me, with my Swedish heritage, all together on a sunny day. What a vivid reminder that it really is "a small world after all."

Thrill Killer may tell you to avoid sharing Jesus. Don't listen to him even one more second; he's just trying to keep as many people as he can in spiritual captivity. There really is no greater high than letting God use you to change another person's life. This thrill's for you—and for the rest of the world too.

For personal or group study guides and leader support resources, go to www.ThrillOnline.net.

AFTERWORD

The awesome thing about a brush with death is that it gives you a new appreciation for life. A young deckhand on a commercial fishing boat in Bristol Bay had just helped tie up his boat to ours as we waited for the next opening to go after Alaskan salmon. While walking on the narrow ledge beside the cabin, he suddenly slipped and plunged into the bone-chilling waters. He had no life jacket and the fast-ebbing tide quickly swept him away from the boat and into serious trouble.

The captain knew he couldn't untie the boat and retrieve the young man before he would drown, so he grabbed a line and tossed it with all his might toward the desperate crewman. The end of the line didn't land within reach of the flailing arms. As the captain quickly coiled the rope for another throw, he knew it was his last chance. He took careful aim and this time hit the man's head. The desperate young man lunged for the line and managed to grasp the last few inches of the only thing that could save him.

Several other deckhands pulled him in as he clung to his *lifeline* in the very literal sense of the word. We soon had him back on deck. Fishing was forgotten as a spontaneous celebration ensued.

Many of us have slipped from solid footing and are being swept away by the deadly currents of spiritual deception. But the Captain of our Souls has thrown us a line comprised of the truths covered in this book. Grasp and cling to them as if your life depended on it—because it does!

If you find yourself drifting off in the future or in danger of sinking, reach for the Bible, this book, an honest friend or any other source of truth from God and let Him pull you to safety.

Enter into the Thrill He has waiting for you!

Join the celebration!

SHARE THE THRILL

God can use you to reach others who feel that "normal is not enough." At www.ThrillOnline.net you can access resources to help you lead with confidence. Share the Thrill at **www.ThrillOnline.net**.

SPEAKING

Karl speaks at churches and leadership conferences around the country and is available to share the message of "Thrill" at your event. Visit **www.ThrillOnline.net** for more information.

COACHING

Let us coach and equip you with practical tools to lead your family, small groups, men's and women's studies. Visit **www.ThrillOnline.net** to download the available tools.

DOWNLOADS

Download Thrill Study Guides, videos and other free resources at **www.ThrillOnline.net**.

ABOUT LIFELANE180

Lifelane180 invites you to join a spiritual revolution. I've written *Thrill: When Normal is Not Enough* to establish and expand our mission. To awaken a spiritual culture within the church that reaches the world.

--Karl Clauson, Founder

VISIT WWW.LIFELANE180.COM

Blogs. Resources. 180OneDays.
Conference and Speaking Schedule.

Join the Team @ www.Lifelane180.com